THE WEIGHT OF A FEATHER

A Mother's Journey Through the Opiate Crisis

Lynda Hacker Araoz

NEW YORK

LONDON • NASHVILLE • MELBOURNE • VANCOUVER

The Weight of a Feather
A Mother's Journey Through the Opiate Addiction Crisis

Published in New York, New York, by Morgan James Publishing. Morgan James is a trademark of Morgan James, LLC. www.MorganJamesPublishing.com

The Morgan James Speakers Group can bring authors to your live event. For more information or to book an event visit The Morgan James Speakers Group at www.TheMorganJamesSpeakersGroup.com.

"Stand By Me"

Words and Music by Jerry Leiber, Mike Stoller and Ben E. King
Copyright (c) 1961 Sony/ATV Music Publishing LLC Copyright Renewed
All Rights Administered by Sony/ATV Music Publishing LLC, 424 Church Street, Suite 1200, Nashville, TN 37219
International Copyright Secured All Rights Reserved
Reprinted by Permission of Hal Leonard LLC

This book is based on the author's experience and memories of certain events and conversations. Names and some minor details have been changed to protect individuals' privacy.

ISBN 9781683509196 paperback
ISBN 9781683509219 hardcover
ISBN 9781683509202 eBook
Library of Congress Control Number: 2017919479

Cover Design by:
Rachel Lopez
www.r2cdesign.com

Interior Design by:
Chris Treccani
www.3dogcreative.net

In an effort to support local communities, raise awareness and funds, Morgan James Publishing donates a percentage of all book sales for the life of each book to Habitat for Humanity Peninsula and Greater Williamsburg.

Get involved today! Visit
www.MorganJamesBuilds.com

To Martin

Table of Contents

PREFACE

People often ask me why I have written this book. It's a logical question. Why would someone choose to go back and revisit the darkest period of her life? Why not just slam the door on that chapter, turn the key in the lock and move on?

The quick answer to that question is that a couple of years beyond where this book ends, I began to feel an inner tension that nagged at me and I realized that I could not walk away from my experience when I knew that thousands of others were going through an experience in some ways similar to mine. At the very least, I wanted them to feel some sense of camaraderie, to feel less alone, to know that someone else had traveled that same road and found light at the end of the tunnel.

By the time my son became addicted to opiates, I had already earned a Master's degree in Social Work, had worked several years in the field and had even helped develop a drug use prevention program in the school where I worked at the time. You would think that my background might have prepared me for the ordeal that lay ahead, that I would have had some special advantage in navigating my way through the system. Unfortunately, that was not the case. I had no idea of the devastation that opiate addiction would cause in our lives until it struck us like a tsunami nor did I ever anticipate the number of obstacles we'd encounter over and over again in trying to find a solution. By sharing some of the pitfalls in our path, I hope that I can provide some direction for change and help pave a smoother road to treatment and recovery. I think we can do better. I think we *must* do better.

And finally, though I never found a place for it in the book itself, there are a few thoughts I wanted to share with those who have just started on the road to recovery. It is a pivotal moment!—at the same time scary and exciting. It reminds me of a statue I once saw of the Roman god Janus who was considered the god of doorways and beginnings. He had two faces, one that looked back at the past and another that looked on to the future, and it seemed to me that the faces of Janus were a lot like the challenges of recovery: one face looking toward a bright future and another looking back at a dark past. To the face looking forward I say this: My heartfelt congratulations and may your new life be filled with strength, promise and contentment! To the face looking backward, I say this: Wounds heal, relationships mend and some things are meant to just remain in the rubble of the past. Shake the dust off your feet and prepare yourself to meet the people and opportunities that lie ahead. Remember that God loves you and thousands of unseen hands are applauding you. Two of those hands are mine.

ACKNOWLEDGEMENTS

My thanks to Morgan James Publishing and Guideposts for helping this book become a reality and to Michele McKay-Aynsworth and Kathleen Turley for their valuable suggestions and friendship. I'd also like to extend my thanks to Scott and Penny for their faithful support and to Rigo, whose sense of humor can always lighten up any dark corner. A special thanks to Carlos for his love, patience and encouragement throughout the writing of this book.

*He shall cover thee with his feathers, and under his wings
shalt thou trust....*
Psalm 91:4 (KJV)

Stand by Me

The beginning of it all is somewhat of a muddle to me, but if I have to start somewhere I think it would be with a phone call in the middle of the night. Actually, it was my husband Jim who picked up the first phone call, and he had the good sense to let me sleep for a while before waking me up. So I woke up to the news that our son Daniel had been in an accident. Driving while intoxicated. The police report was confusing. He had swiped a few cars, gotten into a fight, tried to leave the scene of the accident, the police were going to call back later. Is he OK? Is he in the hospital?

No, he said. Apparently, he's in jail.

I answered the next phone call. By this time, I was screamingly awake. Things still seemed muddled—there were conflicting reports, the police said. But some things were crystal clear. Daniel was going to be arraigned the next morning in city court—you need to be there. I was somehow prepared for the rest—his license was suspended, his car was impounded, he was not injured, he had spent the night in jail.

But he had one more thing to add, the thing that blasted me through some kind of barrier into another world. "You need to call your lawyer," he said, "because besides everything else that happened, your son also hit a pedestrian."

It's funny, but my initial reaction was to his comment about the lawyer rather than the news about the pedestrian. *Who do you think we are? We're not people who have a lawyer, like some people who have a dentist or a doctor or a dry-cleaning service. My lawyer? Who would that be—the pudgy attorney who was at our house closing whose name I can't even remember? A distant cousin who used to probate wills that I haven't talked to in years? Of course, we don't have a lawyer because we're not the kind of people who need a lawyer.* And then I remembered the pedestrian.

"Is he OK?" I asked.

"Still too early to know; he's still in the hospital."

By morning it occurred to me how completely unprepared I was for what lay ahead. The only time I had been in court was for a ticket because my headlight was out, and this was in our little local court. I had to go online to find the location of the city court, and as I looked in my closet, I realized that I wasn't even sure about how one dresses for court. I was in such a state of shock that I couldn't so much as remember the rule whether it is better to overdress or underdress when in doubt. I opted for overdress.

Turns out I was wrong. I entered the court alone because Jim was still circling the courthouse looking for a parking place, and a man in a uniform ushered me toward the first row. Behind me was a row of benches with little groups of people scattered here and there.

Whole families were there, baby carriages and all. *Who brings kids to an arraignment?* I wondered, but then this was all new to me, so maybe that was par for the course.

It didn't take me long to realize that I was the only one in the first row who didn't have a briefcase, and it occurred to me that I had been mistaken as an attorney. With an apologetic wave to the others, I moved back to where I apparently belonged—with the other family members waiting for the whole process to begin. Jim arrived and later another man joined us on the bench. He seemed to be the most animated person in the room, and I instinctively liked him. He introduced himself and handed me his card. His card had a little dark figure which I recognized immediately—the man from the Get Out of Jail Free card in Monopoly. He was a bail bondsman. I struggled to remember what I knew about bail and came up with nothing. It hadn't even occurred to me before leaving home to stop at an ATM, to even think about money. But I felt somehow comforted having someone around who knew the ropes, and I confidently trusted in the kindness of strangers, having no other option. As we waited, he gave us a preview of what would happen in the next half hour or so. Since he was apparently a regular in the courtroom, I asked him if he could recommend an attorney for a DWI case. He scrolled through his phone and came up with two names and numbers which I scribbled on an envelope which I found in my purse. Good lawyers who won't cost you an arm and a leg if you know what I mean, he said. Of course, I didn't know, I didn't know anything about this, but I nodded, grateful for his help.

Eventually, the judge appeared and sometime later, a door opened and a line of men in orange jump suits shuffled in and sat on a special bench in front. They seemed a ragged crew—huddled shoulders, unkempt hair, stubbled chins, eyes fixed on the floor. I cringed at the sight of them, stunned by the visual image of my own son in handcuffs standing there among them. "Which one is yours?" my new friend whispered and I quickly counted down the line.

"The fourth one," I said, "the young kid."

"Hopefully they won't set the bail too high him being so young and all," he said casually, and again I nodded although I had no idea what might be a low or a high bail. And while we waited for Daniel's turn to go before the judge, he gave me a little background on each person. The judge, the DA, the public defender. Labels from a TV show, not my life, but I was all ears now. When it was Daniel's turn, the bail bondsman gently nudged me and said, "Since your son is under age, you can go up and stand with him, you know. Go on, it will work to his benefit." *Why?* I wondered, but I immediately got up and headed for the little gate that would let me into the inner sanctum, the judge and sinners. A clerk opened the door for me as I approached, and then I took my place next to my son who was still handcuffed and looked as if he needed a good night's sleep. There was a lot of mumbling back and forth about the amount of bail and the injured pedestrian, and in the end, the district attorney won out for a higher bail. The public defender then turned her attention to Daniel and began giving him an explanation of what lay ahead. It dawned on me that I should be paying more attention and get beyond the shock that I was standing next to a familiar face in a convict suit. Whether it was the shock or the fact that I was functioning on only a few hours sleep, I found the whole thing hard to follow. For all I knew, she could have been reading him the Declaration of Independence and I wish to God she had been because whether I realized it or not, this was my introduction into a whole new world, a world that would soon be made up of probation officers, judges, lawyers, counselors and social service people of all shapes and sizes. For the rest of the day Ben E. King's song "Stand by Me" rattled through my brain:

When the night has come

And the land is dark

And the moon is the only light we'll see

No I won't be afraid, no I won't be afraid

Just as long as you stand, stand by me

Little did I know that would become my theme song for the next six years.

Down the Rabbit Hole

D espite the anxiety of that first incident, I still thought of Daniel as someone who had veered off the right track, not gone off on the wrong track altogether. After all, I had grown up in a household of brothers at a time when it was not unheard of to travel any long distance with a six pack on the passenger seat just to keep you company. My brothers wrapped cars around telephone poles, knocked over signs and mailboxes, even got into a few drunken fights. I still suspect that some of my pet kittens who suddenly disappeared from one day to the next found their fates under the wheels of my brothers' cars. Not good, not good at all. But there were no DWIs, no probation officers, no court cases. They each left behind them a trail of gnarled cars but nothing more. And, one by one, each of them moved on to another phase and left all of that behind. You ever wonder why you don't recognize so many fellow alumni at your college reunions? Maybe one of the reasons is that the last time you saw them they were at some frat house playing drinking games or passed out on a couch somewhere. And now here they were, ten years, twenty years later, doctors, lawyers and entrepreneurs, dressed in neatly pressed chinos and matching outfits talking about investments and trips to the Bahamas.

Sure, I had watched my older brothers go through their drinking phase, had listened to their arguments with my parents, had seen their wrecked cars, had even gone to the hospital to visit on at least one occasion. I knew the whole thing was like a scary roller coaster ride. But I fully believed that like any ride, it came to an end. Hold your breath, hang on tight and when you open your eyes again, it will all be over.

Or so I thought. Actually, I thought that the whole incident with the pedestrian was going to be the end of the ride. After all, you put your hand near the fire and get burned once, do you go ahead and do it again? In Daniel's case, the answer would be yes. Again and again and again.

What does it take for you to "get it"? It was a question that I posed to Daniel over and over again. One time late at night we received a phone call from the mother of one of Daniel's friends. Her son and Daniel had found a couple of bottles of whiskey at the house and Daniel was drunk. So drunk in fact that she thought we should take him to a hospital. Which we did. He was so wasted we could hardly get him out of the car, in fact, had to get a wheel chair to get him from the car into the emergency room. He stayed there overnight and in the morning when we went to get him, he was still in the hospital bed, his body covered with little circular white pads and wires.

"Look at me," he said, gesturing to the wires all over his body. "I freaked out when I woke up this morning and saw all this. How did this happen? I don't remember anything." It was a phrase we had heard before. How did the lamp get broken? *I don't know. I don't remember anything.* Why is there glass all over the floor? What about that hole in the wall? *I don't know anything about it.* And at first, I thought this response was just a way to avoid taking responsibility. But eventually, I came to the realization that there were times when he really *did not* remember. He was not only drinking heavily; he was having blackouts. In fact, some of my most vivid memories were of incidents which Daniel didn't remember at all.

One day I came home from work and found Daniel and Jim engaged in a heated argument. Daniel had been drinking, he was getting belligerent, things were escalating. I immediately felt that terrible gut-wrenching ache that comes when two people you love are at odds with one another. Stop this. Go somewhere else. Get away from each other. I knew enough about Daniel at that point to know that there was no point in talking to him after he had been drinking. He was not reasonable when he was under the influence, he was incapable of seeing anyone else's point of view, he had a hairline trigger for anger. "Stop this," I yelled again to no one in particular. "Drop it. Go somewhere else."

I had actually hoped that each of them would storm off into different rooms of the house, slam the door perhaps, and things would cool off. But instead Daniel darted out the front door.

Jim and I stood there shaking for a few minutes, and then I went outside to look for Daniel. He was nowhere to be found.

I immediately panicked. "We can't let him wander around the neighborhood in that state," I said. "We need to go find him."

"He'll never get in the car with me at this point," Jim responded and I knew he was right. So I got into my car and began to drive around the neighborhood. No sign of him anywhere. I was about to give up altogether when I saw him scurry across a neighbor's back yard. I quickly pulled the car to the side of the road and jumped out. "Daniel!" I yelled. He turned around, looked briefly at me and then headed off in the opposite direction. He ambled through one neighbor's back yard, then a second and in the third neighbor's yard, he headed toward the woods at the back of their property. If there is any grace in this universe, those neighbors would have been watching the evening news, engaged in a family argument, surfing the internet or doing *anything* other than looking out their back windows that day, because if they were, they would have seen a woman dressed in a beige linen suit and heels chasing through their yard after a disheveled young man, his jacket half off, stumbling over anything that happened to be in his path.

Eventually I caught up with him in the woods. He was, at the time, dangling half-way to the ground, his jacket snagged on a bush. As much as he tugged on the jacket, it would not come loose. I stood next to him, out of breath, and simply said, "Daniel, you have to come home."

Surprisingly, he didn't give me a hard time about that. I helped him out of his jacket, pulled the jacket from the bush and slung it over my shoulder. He tried to walk with me, but he kept stumbling over everything along the way. "Here," I said, draping his arm over my shoulder. "Hang on and let's get you out of here."

And in this way, we maneuvered our way through the woods, stumbling over roots and rocks, circumventing fallen trees, pulling back bushes and branches and finally made it back out to the road and to my car. Perhaps I have watched too many war movies, but the image that sticks in my mind is not so much as a mother and a son, but an army man who goes back for a wounded comrade hoping to pull him out of harm's way. It's funny but I remember this incident almost as if I were an observer rather than a participant in the whole scenario. Daniel, on the other hand, by the next morning didn't remember it at all.

Alcoholic? Addict? Those words didn't even cross my mind at the time. After the accident, Daniel went to court-ordered alcohol counseling, and we redoubled our efforts to point out the dangers of alcohol using any means possible. We made sure there was no alcohol in the house and finally convinced him to get rid of the empty liquor bottles that he had displayed in his room as if they were trophies of some kind. We were constantly pushing newspapers articles across the table to Daniel. See? See what happens to people who drink and drive? If you don't learn from your own mistakes, learn from others. During this time, a student who had been a couple of years ahead of Daniel in school got in a car accident driving back to his college campus and ended up killing three people, including his best friend who was with him at the time. It was on the front page of the newspaper, the talk of the town. What a terrible tragedy for everyone. Drinking and driving. See? See? Nothing good comes of it. And Daniel would heartily agree. "Damn, he'll have to live with that for the rest of his life," he remarked.

Apparently he *got it* on one level, but somehow it didn't make enough of an impact to change his behavior. So the fact that Daniel ended up with a DWI that first day in court and had his license suspended was in some ways a blessing. It would keep him off the road. It would keep him and everybody else safe at least for a while.

Of course, in other ways it was a curse. There are ripple effects to a DWI, especially when you live in the country. No license means no transportation. No transportation means you are constantly relying on other people to get you where you need to go. Jim and I both worked, so we were either taking time off from work or shelling out money for rides. And of course, the only people who were available to provide those rides were other people who didn't seem to have anything else going on in their lives. We were relying on the unreliable.

Daniel finished his six weeks of mandated alcohol counseling. His final report indicated that he had engaged in treatment and was a good participant which meant that we no longer had to spend two or three evenings a week driving him to an agency forty-five minutes away, waiting in the car until he finished his session and then driving him back home again. Other than that, nothing else in our life seemed to change. He may have engaged in alcohol treatment, but we suspected that it was not the only thing that he was engaged in during those six weeks.

Nevertheless, we plugged onward. Daniel was still in school at the time, and we set our focus on making sure he graduated. At one time, I had pictured myself visiting colleges with Daniel, waiting for admission letters in the mail, loading up the car with suitcases and blankets and driving him off to the start of a professional career. The bar was set much lower at this point; in fact, it was only inches off the ground. Getting him out of bed in the morning and out the door—hopefully to school—was as much as we could handle, and we weren't being too successful at even this. Still we had hope. He had, after all, passed all the state exams, an extraordinary feat we thought, considering the fact that we had never seen him with a textbook in his hand. But we were on thin ice. Calls from teachers all reported the same thing: smart kid, but he doesn't do anything and is in danger of failing. Though this threw me into a panic, it didn't seem to bother Daniel at all. And in the end, he failed just one course, but a course he needed to graduate, a course only offered first semester. *So sorry.* But we were determined to trudge onward. We found an equivalent course at the local community college and enrolled him with the school's full approval. Daniel could still graduate in June. We bought the textbook, read a few chapters ahead so we could perhaps engage Daniel in conversation around the subject matter. But getting him to the college each week was just as hard as getting him to school in the morning, and by June it was clear that he would be one of the few from his class who would not be graduating that year.

Oh, sure. Natural consequences. Free will. Personal decision-making. Whatever. I took it as a personal affront. As an educator, I had always been a champion of the underdog. The underprivileged, the immigrants, the troublemakers, the mentally challenged all found a place under my wing, and they all went on to caps and gowns and a thin piece of paper that said they were ready to face the world. What I was able to do for others, I was not able to do for my own son. Of course, there was an important difference: those people had actually tried, had wanted to succeed, were willing to grab onto a helping hand, make the effort. Daniel did not fit into this category at all, and this made me feel even worse. I felt I had failed on a colossal level.

"I am not going out this weekend," I announced to my husband a few days before graduation. "I have a lot of things to do here at home." Of course, that was only partly true. The real truth was that I couldn't stand the thought of driving past the high school parking lot filled with cars and seeing the chairs set up for the graduation ceremony. I wasn't planning to drive past house after house in the neighborhood and see the blue and silver balloons and *Congratulations!* signs on front lawns. The rest of the family went on with their usual routines. I stayed at home and moped.

By Sunday I had changed my mind. I woke up that morning with the image of an old country church in my mind, one that I recognized as located in a small hamlet in the northern part of the county. "I'm going to church," I told Jim as he sat down for breakfast.

"You want to ride together?" he asked.

"You go on ahead," I said. "I'm not planning to go to our church."

He raised an eyebrow and simply said, "Suit yourself."

That was exactly what I was planning to do. I was not going to go to a place where people *knew* me, would approach me, ask how I was doing or even—horror of horrors!—actually make a mistake and congratulate me on my son's graduation. Although I had never been to the church I planned on going to, I was fairly confident that I wouldn't know anyone and was expecting nothing more than a half-empty church and a comforting message along the lines of "All will be well. The storm will pass."

Well, the church was half-empty. I got that part right. I was dead wrong about everything else. The theme of the sermon was graduation. New beginnings! Bright futures! I squirmed in my hard, wooden pew and wondered what in the world I was thinking in not just staying home. I thought the service would end with the sermon and I could make a quick escape, but instead the minister invited anyone who wanted to pray to come on forward. I groaned as I saw people lining up. The first one to step up to the microphone was, of all people, the superintendent of Daniel's school, and he dutifully prayed for all the graduates and their families. Everyone who went forward followed suit. *Who are these people anyway?* I wondered. Christians are being persecuted in foreign countries, soldiers are risking their lives abroad, poverty is rampant in the world and we are praying for *high school graduates* (who by the way seemed to be absent from the church on that day, probably recovering from celebrating the previous night)? This may not be the Miss America pageant, but couldn't we give a little lip service to *world peace* instead of praying for people who seem to be doing quite well on their own without any help whatsoever? I was just about to scoot out of my pew and sneak out the back when the last man in line picked up the microphone. "I'd like to pray for someone in this room," he paused and scanned the room, "and I ask that God send that person a very present help." That was it. Short and sincere. I took a quick look around at the smiling faces in the room and decided that prayer had to be for me. And even if it wasn't, I claimed it for my own, and with the organ thundering in the background, I took that opportunity to dash out.

The next day Daniel was scheduled to begin a new program of alcohol counseling. He had had a brush with the law and was mandated to another several months of counseling at a center in a different city, one that I was not familiar with. I dropped him off at the center and drove around looking for a place to settle in for an hour and a half; it didn't make sense to drive home and then turn around and come back. What I found were bars and darkened store fronts. It seemed somehow unspeakably indecent to spend time in a bar while your son is in alcohol counseling, so I kept on driving until I found a plaza with a used bookstore that had a light on inside. I rapped on the door and peered in. "Are you open?" I asked.

"Not really," said a woman from behind a stack of books. "I'm just working late. But you're welcome to look around if you'd like. I'll be here for a while."

And so I browsed, and since I had more than an hour left to kill, I browsed everything—history, mystery, fiction, non-fiction. It didn't matter much to me. It was warm and pleasant there in the shop and I wasn't looking for anything special. And then a few minutes before I was about to leave, I spotted it…a tattered book cover with these words on its spine: *A very present help,* the very same words the man had used the day before. It seemed such a quirky coincidence that I bought the book without even bothering to look inside.

Turns out that the book was a series of personal accounts put together by Guideposts back in the 1980s. Fascinating stories of people who miraculously survived plane crashes, predators, fires and storms. I was so intrigued by it that I finished reading it within a day. Above all, I found it *encouraging.* After all, if God was in the business of miracles, there was no reason that Daniel couldn't be his next customer.

Lions and Tigers and Bears, Oh My!

We soon fell into a routine again. I would drop Daniel off for alcohol counseling and would go to the used bookstore or hang out under a street light that I discovered was bright enough to read under. Nothing else seemed to change. "What do you do there anyway?" I would ask Daniel on occasion.

"Oh, we watch movies, or people just tell their stories." And sometimes he would tell me some of those stories…failed marriages, broken commitments, lost jobs, squandered fortunes. He felt genuinely sorry for the others in his group, but never seemed to make the connection, to recognize that the path the others had taken was the same path he was currently on.

By that time, I realized that drinking was no longer the main issue. People like to say in retrospect they could see all the signs of drug use. I didn't need retrospect. All the signs were right out there in my face. The occasional smell of marijuana, a clip sitting on the arm of a lawn chair, a pack of zigzag rolling papers. It astounded me that he didn't have the sense to even hide things before we arrived home. And the lies began: *What? I don't smell anything. I don't know how it got there. Must have been someone else who left it there.*

Someone else? Who was in the house when we were gone? *Why would someone bring a pack of rolling papers to my house? Tell me that.* With school over, Daniel had too much time on his hands. He found jobs, but none of them seemed to last long. His ride would show up late, he would wake up late, he had appointments with probation and the court that interfered with work. I had little confidence that his counseling groups were going to change much of anything.

Some things did seem to be changing though. What seemed to change was that Daniel was becoming more secretive about his activities. We had entered into another phase. At the same time, my husband and I also became more vigilant about our own affairs. We changed our bank accounts to on-line statements and destroyed old statements, put passwords on our computers, kept checkbooks well-hidden at all times. I practically slept with my pocketbook. Would Daniel have stolen anything? I don't know. Probably. The foundation of trust had been broken and we weren't going to take chances. Anything important was locked in the glove compartment or the trunk of our cars.

The arguments continued, but Daniel became increasingly more belligerent and defiant. We set rules. He would agree to them and then break them. We discovered things missing from the house, things broken, cigarette butts in saucers, burn holes in the carpet and on the upholstered furniture.

"I thought we agreed there was no smoking in the house," we'd say.

"I don't know how they got there," he'd respond. "Maybe one of my brother's friends."

His younger brother Travis. Our other son was finishing middle school. He had one foot in childhood and the other foot in adolescence. We knew his friends. When they came to the house, they still put together Legos on occasion, they played video games, they watched sports events on TV. Although a few of them had taken on the swagger of a teenager, they still carried an aura of innocence. In the morning after a sleep-over, I would still find them watching cartoons for God's sake. I constantly agonized about the effect all of this was having on Travis. At first when we saw an argument brewing, we would send him up to his room to watch TV or do his homework. But who were we kidding? Who can do homework when a battle is raging on the floor beneath you? And as time went on, he would race downstairs at the start of an argument, no longer willing to stand on the sidelines. It became a family free-for-all. Even the dog joined in, barking and jumping from one place to another. The truth is that Travis sensed what we already knew: our household, our family, our whole routine of life was unraveling. I think on some level he hoped that he could save us all from each other, restore order in a house that had become hopelessly chaotic, rescue us from the doom that awaited us. Cartoons come to life, a Marvel hero in action.

I wish he could've rescued us, that anyone could've rescued us because at that point anger had become a driving force in the house, a whirlwind that uprooted everything in its path, a fire that ignited everything around it.

Things continued to disappear at home, at first just minor things. A nuisance, we thought, misplaced things that would show up sooner or later. When larger things disappeared, we didn't bother looking for an explanation. As sick as it made us feel, we knew what was happening. When we confronted Daniel, he denied any responsibility whatsoever; someone must have broken into the house, he offered. There have been a lot of robberies in our neighborhood lately, he would say. That explanation did nothing to appease our anger at his behavior. One Christmas Eve while wrapping presents, I suddenly discovered that a television and a CD player were missing; another time a ring disappeared off my dresser. More accusations, more denials, more frustrations, more anger.

The storm broke when Travis came back from a sleepover with friends and discovered things missing from his room. He was beyond himself with rage. We hoped for some explanation other than the obvious. Had he possibly lent them to a friend? Had Daniel simply borrowed them? But no one bothered to ask these questions. Things had disappeared from Travis's room before, but they had been small things—a controller, a video game and we had somehow gotten beyond this by replacing them, putting a lock on Travis's door, having a stern talk with Daniel. But this was something different—his door had been broken open and his television, the one he had saved for and bought for himself, was gone. He felt violated. "I'll kill him," he said, his voice quivering with pain and rage. "I'll kill the sonofabitch." He went racing toward Daniel's room, and I thanked God Daniel was not there at the time. Travis threw his chair against the wall, in one swoop cleaned everything off his desk and was reaching for his lamp when I grabbed his arm.

"Stop," I yelled. I took a moment to catch my breath. "Go back to your room, grab a bag and a few things for the night. Take anything that is important to you, put it in a box and bring it out to my car. We're leaving."

He was still shaking with rage, and I was barely holding on myself. Jim, who had followed me upstairs, looked at the things on the floor and looked at me as if to ask, what is going on? I simply shrugged. I didn't know what I was doing—I only knew that Travis had been pushed beyond the breaking point. He had never used language like this, had never acted like this. This raw explosion of anger coming from him scared me, and I shuddered to think what would have happened if Daniel had been there in his room at the time. We weren't going to resolve this by replacing the TV, by fixing the door, by soothing reassuring words. We were beyond that. We needed to get out of there, at least for the time being.

I grabbed an old sweatshirt and a few odds and ends and went to my car to make room in the trunk. Travis shuffled out with a couple of bags, we settled them in the back and he got into the front seat.

We sat in silence for a while, each lost in our own thoughts, and I simply drove, still livid at what Daniel had done, still aching for Travis, keenly aware of the fact that Daniel had broken through yet another boundary. *How could he do such a thing?* I wondered over and over again. *How could he?*

Finally, it was Travis who broke the silence. "Where are we going, anyway?" he asked.

I looked up at the next sign, noticed we were already near Springfield and said simply, "Cape Cod. We're going to Cape Cod."

I hadn't actually thought about it, but on the other hand, it wasn't a bad option. Years ago, we had spent a couple of summers there. It was a place that held good memories for us, a place that belonged to a time when we were all safe, a place that hadn't been spoiled by all the chaos of the past couple of years.

"In winter? Who goes to Cape Cod in the winter?"

"I don't know. I guess we'll see when we get there. Personally, I have always wanted to go to Cape Cod in winter. No traffic jams, crowded beaches…."

He simply rolled his eyes. And then he vented for the next 100 miles. He exploded with anger, he wept with frustration, and he asked me the same question I had asked myself over and over: "Why can't you make this all stop? Why don't you *do* something to make this stop?"

And he rambled on. "Our house is filled with low life; our lives are a mess. I hate Daniel, I hate everything about him. Call the police on him. Throw him out of the house. Do something. I wish you had never adopted him. I wish you had never adopted me."

That last statement cut me to the quick, but I just drove and let him talk. And although he never actually said it, I felt the nagging accusation: If you're my mother, why can't you protect me? Why can't you take care of this? Eventually Travis dozed off, I turned on the radio and we drove toward the Cape.

Of course, what he didn't know was that I *had* tried. I had called the police on several occasions when things got out of hand. I had talked with *dozens* of people hoping to find a solution. I had given Daniel money to move out, I had sent him to visit a friend in another part of the state with the hopes that he might start a new life there. I was paying for him to go to an anger management group; Jim and I had gone to counseling with him. I had done everything I could think to do, but nothing seemed to work out. More than once Daniel had told me that he was moving in with a friend, even packed a bag as if he were really going to move out, but before we ever had a chance to catch our breath, he was always back, and the whole scenario would start again. I couldn't blame Travis for being frustrated; I was as frustrated as he was.

I woke him after we crossed the bridge onto the Cape and we spent a little time visiting a few of the many hotels with vacancy signs (after all, who *does* go to the Cape in winter?), trying to decide which one had an indoor pool, a game room, the best view of the ocean. Now that we were five hours away from home, it was beginning to feel a little more like an adventure than an escape and that was a good thing. After a quick meal of fish and chips at a restaurant we had gone to years ago, we bundled up and walked the beach. We tried to fly a kite we found tangled in a bush, threw stones into the ocean and scratched drawings on the wet beach with a stick we had found along the way. We remembered other trips to the Cape—bike rides along the beach, the time the seagulls flew off with our lunch and the warm summer nights we would walk to Emack & Bolio's, the best ice cream shop on the Cape. Occasionally we even laughed as we talked about one thing or another. We didn't say a word about what had happened at home. When it became too windy and cold to bear, we found a little shack still open, shared a lobster and clams and went back to the hotel room. Travis spent some time surfing the TV channels and settled on a comic movie we had seen years before. We had a few good laughs through the beginning scenes and then suddenly he was asleep. I looked at him, lying there so peacefully, his hand curled under his chin, his characteristic sleeping position since he had been a small child. It was a tender moment for me, and I lingered in it—how simple it was to love a child when that emotion wasn't tangled up with so many other conflicting emotions.

In the morning, we had breakfast and started the long drive home. We spent most of the ride home once again lost in our own thoughts. I dreaded the thought of going back home, I suspect we both did. We hadn't solved anything, I couldn't even say that we had put a patch on the wound, but for a few hours we had connected; we had a chance to revert back to who we once were.

The truth was that Daniel's problem had consumed us, had hijacked our lives. At the beginning I used to rationalize spending so much time with him with the simple parable—when a sheep is lost, doesn't the shepherd leave the flock to go in search of the lost sheep? The answer to that question is, of course, yes. But that only works out neatly if the first sheep is found promptly and can be guided back to the flock. How much time does the shepherd devote to rescuing that sheep before he decides that it is more important to save the flock? By trying to rescue one sheep was I, in the end, sacrificing another? As far as being a shepherd—or a mother for that matter—I wasn't exactly a shining success.

One thing that came out of Travis's talk during our trip to the Cape was that our house had become a haven for what he called "low life" on a regular basis. The idea of strangers in our house while we were away at work was a constant aggravation and the source of more than one argument, but until that point, I thought (or maybe just hoped) that other people came to our house only occasionally. If there was any truth to what Travis was saying, people were coming and going in and out of our house on a regular basis, and moreover, their activity was not restricted just to Daniel's room or the living room. Jim was appalled when I told him, and together we determined to stop this ebb and flow in and out of the house. We started devising ways to come home during the day and what we found only heightened our concern. Who were these people anyway? They were not the friends of Daniel that we had come to know over the years—kids who had played soccer with him, kids who came to his birthday parties and went to school with him. For the most part, as we soon learned, these were not people who greeted you when you came in the door, looked you in the eye and introduced themselves. Upon seeing us, most would quickly gather up anything left on a nearby table and hightail it toward the front door as fast as possible. Others would linger as if indifferent to our arrival in the house. As Travis had pointed out so vividly, these were people who were up to no good.

If we couldn't solve the problem with Daniel, at the very least we could take back control of our own house. And we did it with a vengeance. We were beyond social norms. "Time to clear out," we'd say when we encountered a stranger in the house, and if the person didn't move, we would become a little more abrupt. "Now! Take your stuff with you and don't bother coming back here." Sometimes they would mumble that they were just leaving anyway, but other times there were arguments. Daniel invited me, they'd say. "Well, the last time I checked he wasn't paying the mortgage, so I'm inviting you now and I'm inviting you to leave. And do us both a favor and don't come back here or I'll be calling the police next time." Occasionally strangers came to the door asking for money. Daniel owes me fifty, a hundred, even two hundred dollars, they'd say. I don't want to make trouble for you and your family, but I want my money. At this point I had such anger and frustration built up in me that this didn't even intimidate me. I was so fed up with it all that I could have faced an army of thugs. "You threatening me and my family?" I'd ask. *Well, bring it on.*

Of course, none of this sat well with Daniel. How can you talk to my friends like that? he'd ask. Friends? You call these people friends? If they're your friends, go to their house and don't invite them to mine.

And believe it or not, eventually people stopped coming. We were still losing the war, but at least we had won a battle. But it was no time to let down our guard and celebrate. A phone call one day alerted us to a problem that had been lurking there on the horizon unbeknown to us for some time.

The pedestrian from the accident? The one we'd heard had sprained his ankle? His family had hired a lawyer and was suing us for a million dollars.

Help, I Need Somebody, Help Not Just Anybody....

The legal suit brought a new whole cast of characters into our world. The insurance company, another lawyer, trips to Boston to meet with the lawyer, to do the deposition. "But this pedestrian, who was walking in the street at 3:00am in the morning on his way to a convenience market. Didn't it occur to anyone that he may have been drinking too?" I asked the lawyer.

He just looked at me and sighed. "I think we all *assume* he had been drinking, was probably on his way to get more beer. However, it's not against the law to get drunk; it's against the law to get drunk and climb into the driver's seat of a car. Once you do that, everything else becomes irrelevant."

Stupid and stupider. Stupider loses and stupid wins. At one point, I left the lawyer's office and went down to the street to put more money in the parking meter. On the way back up in the elevator, I found myself with a tall, lanky young man and a woman who I assumed was his mother. He was literally bouncing up and down in the elevator and prattling on and on about his upcoming good fortune. "I'm figuring that I can pay for my whole college education with this," he said. "Maybe you can even retire, buy a condo in Florida," he told her. He was clearly in a good mood and I might have been tempted to feel happy for him, except for the fact that I noticed we were getting off at the same floor. When the doors opened, he sprinted out and started down the hall, his mother just a few steps behind him; halfway down, he paused and began to limp ever so slightly. His mother caught up to him and he took hold of her arm and they proceeded down the hall, his limp becoming more pronounced with each step. I just stood by the elevator and watched. Sure enough, this was the pedestrian who was suing us. He had found his pot of gold at the end of the rainbow and it was us. Maybe he wasn't so stupid after all.

As alarming as this new development was, it quickly took a back seat to another one. One afternoon I was at home sorting through bills when Daniel suddenly appeared.

"Listen," he said. "There's something I need to tell you." He pulled up a chair next to me and instinctively I braced myself. This was usually the introduction to a comment such as "I need some money" or "I need a ride to an appointment", but something in his tone of voice made me feel this time was different, that this was a lead ball that was about to be thrown into my court. He said nothing for a few minutes and then without any introduction simply blurted out: "I'm addicted to heroin."

A gun went off in my head. I knew he was a user, although I wasn't exactly sure of *what* but somehow the two words together—addict and heroin—caught me off guard. This was the stuff of movies—of strung out people living in grungy apartments, panhandling on the streets, needles and danger. I took a minute to catch my breath and try to picture this in our middle-class world. And then I routinely went through the obvious why, what, where and when questions. The answers were brief and at that point I really didn't dig for details—what I knew already was more than enough for me to handle.

"Well," I said simply, "we need to find you some help." I said that with a false air of confidence since I didn't have the slightest idea of what that might mean. It was as if someone had turned on the engine, but we still sat there idling. We sat there a few more minutes letting it all sink in.

"Well, I'm tired, I going to bed," he said finally, somehow relieved by his confession.

He may have been relieved by this confession, but I was overwhelmed by the weight of it. My son, a heroin addict. My son, a heroin addict. It was as if the words dangled out there in space, unconnected to anything else in my life. I tried to find some solace in his confession. After all, if you can identify the problem, you can solve it. In the medical world, you go through a grueling period of investigation, a doctor comes up with a diagnosis, and even when it's not great—a slipped disc, a cracked rib—you relax because you know that the next step is treatment and resolution.

In the morning, I remembered that Jim had an important appointment that day and decided that this might not be the best moment to share the latest news with him. I called work to let them know I needed the day off and tried to determine what I should do next. I had no background in addiction, I didn't know anyone who was addicted, I didn't know anything about recovery, I knew even less about heroin. There were undoubtedly thousands of parents and professionals in the world who had dealt with this, but I didn't know any of them. This was not my world. In my mind, I scanned through a list of the people I knew intimately and then the people I knew casually and quickly realized that I didn't know anyone who would have the slightest idea how to advise me. So I started making phone calls. "My son just told me that he is a heroin addict," I announced hesitantly to a number of complete strangers over the phone. "What do I do now?" And they all said the same thing, "You need to get him some help. Why don't you make an appointment for him to come in?" And I would breathe a sigh of relief, but every appointment they offered was too far in the future. "But I need help right now," I would say, and they would point out they were booked up and this was the best they could do. This was not good enough. I may not have known exactly what to do, but instinctively I knew that I needed to take some kind of immediate action. When the gun goes off, the race begins and you start moving. In my mind, the gun had gone off.

I flipped through the phone book, I went online. I kept calling. At first it all seemed bizarre, jarring, but as the phone calls went on, I rattled it off as easily as if I were reading it from a script. "My son is a heroin addict. What do I do?" Sure, there was help available, but it was weeks, sometimes even months away. The solution was *counseling*. Half-heartedly I took a few of the appointments offered to me because I felt like I needed a Plan B, while trying to put a Plan A in place. The voices on the other end of the line were mostly kind, sometimes matter of fact, a few times irritated: "Why didn't you call earlier? There are other people who need help too, you know. You're not the only one in this situation." At one point, I talked to a kindly woman who said simply: "You know, it's not enough for you to want help. Does *your son* want help?" She had me there. I didn't know.

Why didn't I know the answer to this? I just *assumed* Daniel told me about his addiction because he wanted help. But maybe there was another motive altogether. Maybe he told me because he was tired of keeping it a secret, tired of coming up with lies and excuses. Maybe the weight of it was too heavy for him, and he just wanted to lessen the load by somehow sharing it with someone else.

Finally, I got through to a therapist we had been to years before, back when Daniel's problems centered around drinking and anger management. We had only gone to see him a few times and it didn't lead to much of a successful outcome, but on the other hand he knew us, we wouldn't waste a whole session going through a series of introductory questions and, more importantly, he agreed to see us the next day.

Naively, I expected that we were on our way to a solution. Not going at full speed, mind you, but at least on our way. I couldn't have been more wrong. The whole session turned into a tug of war. "You need to get some outside help," the therapist would say and Daniel would say, "I can do this on my own. I don't need anyone else's help." And the therapist would say, "If you could do it on your own, you would have done it and you haven't" and Daniel would respond, "Just because I haven't done it in the past, doesn't mean I won't do it in the future." It was an exercise in frustration. We went back one more time, performed the same dance and then gave it up altogether. The gun had gone off, but we were still standing there at the starting line. On to Plan B.

PLANS B AND C AND D, E, F

Plan B, etc. stretched into years. Daniel started back in counseling but it was touch and go. He still couldn't drive so we continued with the age-old dilemma—risk taking off more time from work or risk relying on a stranger to get him to counseling. Over the next few years, we would drive him to four hospitals, five out-patient clinics and two residential placements. We had the door shut in our face so many times, I am surprised my nose is not broken. General hospitals were quick to say they didn't have a detox unit so they couldn't help, and the one hospital with a detox unit was quick to say there were not enough symptoms present to accept Daniel. "Take a look at him," I'd say, as Daniel squirmed in his seat in the waiting room, obviously already feeling cravings. "He needs help." But my pleas fell on deaf ears. "What more do you need? What about doing a drug test? What about admitting him and keeping him under observation for a few more hours and see how that goes?" But that's not the way they did things. There were rules, there were policies, they'd say. And while they were supported by rules and policies, we were being strangled by them. No beds, wrong insurance, pre-admission requirements, not enough symptoms. "Have you tried counseling," they'd ask. I wanted to scream every time I heard that.

Sometime after the announcement that he was a heroin addict, Daniel announced that he was on suboxone, an alternative to heroin. It doesn't get you high, he said, it just keeps you from feeling sick, from going through withdrawal. He obviously saw this as progress, but I had my doubts. It just seemed as if he was continually exchanging one substance for another. And you're not supposed to drink alcohol with it, he added, as if this were just the icing on the cake.

The difference of course was that suboxone was legal, prescribed by a doctor presumably. But not by any doctor as I was to learn, and there were not enough suboxone doctors to keep up with the demand, so there were long waiting lists just to get your foot in the door, and then a whole set of requirements to avoid being shown out the door once you got in. Consequently, tabs or film strips of suboxone were being sold on the street like any other kind of illegal drug. It was currency in the underworld. And when it wasn't available? People got by with a few bags of heroine, which were apparently cheaper and more readily available.

I was determined that if Daniel were to stay on suboxone, he would do it legally. He started with a doctor and a prescription like any other prescription you would fill at your local pharmacy. But somewhere along the way he didn't follow rules and announced one day he been kicked out of treatment and was consequently out of suboxone. Panic set in. How could he possibly mess up something as important as this? The answer was simple: there were mandatory drug tests in order to stay on suboxone and they had detected marijuana on his last drug test. I was livid. I pulled a list of suboxone doctors off the internet and had him call every doctor on the list. Not a single one of them had an opening; the best anyone could offer was a spot on the waiting list. There were a lot of stop-gap efforts—a methadone clinic, a doctor in a far-away city, one crisis after another as we waited for Daniel's name to climb to the top of someone's waiting list.

During one of these emergencies I took Daniel to a community health center that reportedly had a crisis center. Don't picture a luxurious waiting room with comfortable chairs and friendly faces. Picture a place with worn-out faces and cranky kids and a group of chairs that could have been picked off the street. We landed there as a last resort because it seemed that no one—not hospitals nor counselors—could offer any help. Do you have an appointment? the receptionist asked us. "No," I said. *We are in crisis.*" We, and I do mean we, were in crisis because once again Daniel was out of suboxone and was already shaking like a leaf and we had nowhere else to turn. The receptionist took one quick look at him and said, "Third door on the right." And the woman sitting at the desk in that office listened long and hard to our difficulties, made several phone calls, called in a colleague and we all tried to look for a solution.

"This is a major problem in this area," she said with a sigh. "Not enough suboxone doctors." Between the two of them, they came up with a list of suboxone doctors in the area and as I glanced at it, I realized we had already called every one of them except one.

"They're all full. Daniel is already on the waiting list," I said. She called the one doctor I hadn't called and received the same response. "What are we supposed to do now?" I asked.

And she looked me straight in the eye and said, "I hate to have to say this, but I think you know what people do in situations like this." And I knew what she meant: *Buy it on the street.* Buy it on the street? What kind of answer is that? But she tried, she really did. Either she or her colleague would call Daniel or me every week or so and provide us with any lead they could find—a doctor several hours away from us, another doctor who didn't take insurance and charged a king's ransom for just an initial appointment but would guarantee a prescription, a fleeting possibility that their own agency could contract with a doctor who would soon be certified to prescribe suboxone. I immediately grabbed at this possibility. "How soon?" I asked. In a few months. Not soon enough. The end of the line seemed always to stretch further and further away.

Over and over again there would be a glimmer of hope, but it would turn out to be merely that…a glimmer of hope, not a light through the darkness. We had just evolved into another phase which seemed as treacherous as the last phase. And we would see many dark days of desperation—his animated, mine gnawing—before we ever really saw any light.

Oh, the Places You'll Go!

We went through a period where Daniel always seemed to be lost, and I don't mean figuratively lost. Meet me at such and such a place, he'd say, my ride left without me, my ride never came back for me, the guy who was driving me is messed up and I don't want to get in the car with him. And though he always met me in some fairly respectable place—a gas station, a pizza shop, a convenience store—the address was always in a sleazy neighborhood with poorly lit streets, empty except for a few scattered figures who seemed to slink in and out of adjacent alleyways. I wasn't so worried about him being in the right place at the wrong time. I would have been happy with him being in the right place under any circumstances. It just seemed he was in the wrong place on a fairly regular basis. And because I was often the one picking him up, he put me in those places too.

One time while I was waiting for him to arrive at the designated meeting spot, I was suddenly jolted by the beam of a light, then another one, flashing inside my car. I quickly checked my door to make sure it was locked and then suddenly there was a policeman inches from my window with his flashlight shining in my face. "What're you doing here?"

"Waiting for my son."

"What's he doing here?"

"Visiting a friend."

"What's the address? Why isn't he here to meet you?"

"I don't know. Maybe he stopped for a soda or something."

"Do this on a regular basis?"

"No, I just happened to be up this way when he called."

"Did he say where he called from?"

While this whole staccato interchange was going on, the second policeman continued to search my backseat with the beam of his flashlight. Nothing there but a box of books and a bag of groceries, but he was being diligent. And then suddenly Daniel appeared, God love him, looking almost respectable with a can of soda in his hand.

"Oh, oh, sorry," said the policeman as he shut off his flashlight and motioned to his buddy to back off. Wrong place at the right time. "Yeah, sorry," said his buddy as he moved back into the darkness. Apparently, something was scheduled to go on in that parking lot and I was just unlucky enough to park on the set. Who knows what they thought? Just another nice respectable family out slumming it for the evening.

Another time I waited for him in another shady neighborhood, in a parking place around the corner of a brightly lit street with a pizza joint on the corner. Unbeknown to me, a flatbed truck came reeling along the street behind me, cut the corner short and slammed into the driver's side of my car so hard, the car went flying onto the sidewalk in front of the pizza place. It was like being ripped out of the audience and thrown onto a brightly lit stage. The truck disappeared into the night, and I immediately crawled out the passenger side of the car and found myself surrounded by a ring of strangers. "Are you OK?" and "What a sonofabitch," and "Another Hit and Run" they said, along with a bunch of other sympathetic comments that began with "People like that ought to…." I had no idea where these people came from. When I had pulled into the parking place, the whole area had been deserted. A little action on the street and suddenly there was an audience.

Apparently upon seeing a car come flying onto his doorstop, the worker in the pizza joint had called 911 because in a few minutes a police car arrived and the crowd was suddenly gone. Poof! Fastest disappearing act you ever saw in your life. Must be magic in places like this.

And then it was just me and the police of course and then Daniel, who had missed the whole drama. The policeman started to take down information when suddenly a car pulled right into the parking space where my car had once been and out jumped a man waving a newspaper at me. He spoke to me in broken English and for a moment I couldn't imagine how he fit into the whole crazy scenario. But then he thrust a Chinese newspaper in my hand with a string of letters and numbers scribbled on top. I just stared at it for a couple of minutes before it dawned on me; he had followed the truck that had hit me and copied down the license plate. So I nodded and I thanked him and the policeman grabbed the paper out of my hands. "The truck it hide in the park," the man said, which made no sense at all to me, but just as if the police officer had cracked the code, both he and the man sped off in their cars, leaving Daniel, me and my crumpled car alone on stage under the streetlight. The drama had moved elsewhere. And eventually they did find the driver and the truck was in fact hiding in a corner of the park. They verified the license plate and the man with the Chinese newspaper gave the police an eye witness account of the whole event. Oh, the kindness of strangers! There may be a theme developing here.

Another time Daniel wanted to meet me at a local shopping mall. He had caught a ride there and was going to meet up with a girl and hang out with friends. However, he desperately needed money, he had to pay off a debt, he really needed it this time and he was willing to work for it, etc. Yeah, yeah, yeah, it was the same routine. I didn't believe him for a minute. Jim was out of town on a business trip at the time so the ball was in my court. Daniel and I had the same argument over money that we'd had a hundred times before and then he abruptly ended the conversation with "I'll call you in a few minutes when I get there" and he hung up. Minutes went by with no call and I felt relieved. When over an hour passed with no call, I began to feel uneasy about the whole situation. When I called his cell phone, there was no answer. I began to suspect the worst and finally drove to the shopping mall and waited, but there was no sign of him. I called his phone number again and again, but there was no answer. The longer I waited, the more I began to worry. He was never late when he needed money. Something was very wrong with the picture. When my phone rang, I quickly grabbed it, thinking it might be him, but instead it was a stranger's voice. It was the girl he was going to meet. She remembered that he had once called me from her phone and was able to pick out my number from her outgoing calls. Did I know where he was? He had never done this before and she was worried. She and I never met, but for over an hour, she and I collaborated by phone on one plan after another trying to find Daniel. She would stay in the parking lot and I would go out circling through the nearby streets, and then I would circle the parking lot and she would go out looking in another direction. I was about ready to give up altogether when I got another phone call. I quickly grabbed the phone, hoping I would hear Daniel's voice, but once again it was the voice of a stranger.

"There is a young man on my lawn," a female voice said. "He's in bad shape and not very coherent, but when I asked him if there was someone I could call, he gave me this number. Are you his mother?"

She gave me her address, a few directions and fifteen minutes later I was in front of her house. He was, as she had expressed so politely, in bad shape—completely disoriented, physically wasted. I literally had to pull him up off the lawn, and her husband helped me get him into the back seat of the car. It was one of those times when you wonder whether you should give in to your feelings of frustration and disappointment or be thankful that nothing really *really* terrible had happened. Bad as it all was, I figured Daniel would doze off in the back seat and we would make it home without any additional drama. He was safe, I was relieved, and the danger had passed like a storm cloud floating beyond us.

I couldn't have been more wrong. I slowed down at a stop sign on the way home and in a flash Daniel opened the car door, leaped out and ran across four lines of traffic without as much as a glance in either direction. I pulled over to the side of the road and watched as he disappeared into a woods on the far side of the street. I didn't hesitate this time. I had already done a search and rescue through the woods with him, and these woods were much more extensive than the ones I had rescued him from years before. I immediately called the police. And oddly enough, this all seemed to have occurred on the border of two counties, so within minutes police cars from both counties were lined up on both sides of the road. Uniformed men with walkie talkies strolled back and forth giving orders to each other as they staked out a plan to patrol the area from all sides. One of them stopped by my car and I rolled down my window. "Is he armed?" he asked. I just looked at him, stunned by his question.

"No, of course not." And one by one, three different policemen stopped to tell me sternly, "You stay right there in the car. Don't even think about getting out." *Why did they tell me that? Were they planning to have some kind of shoot out?*

And then finally, one of them came back to my car. "Don't you worry," he said, as I rolled down the window again. "We've called in the canine unit. We'll find him one way or another."

I know that was supposed to reassure me, but all I felt was chagrin. So once again I sat and waited and watched as the passing cars slowed down so the passengers could gawk at the whole scene and wonder what in the world had brought out the entire police force from two counties. I wondered if any of them recognized my car or were able to see me through the window as I sat there in my little safety bubble. Eventually an ambulance arrived and I backed up to give it room enough to join the line of police cars.

I kept my eyes fixed on the row of trees at the front of the woods and sure enough, after what seemed to be an eternity, Daniel appeared, his hands over his head and a policeman at each side. I saw them handcuff him and maneuver him across the road. It was like watching a TV show. They took him directly to the ambulance.

The same policeman came back to my car to give me an update. "They're taking him up to…" and he named a hospital a half-hour from there. "He's absolutely smashed," he said, "but he'll be all right. They'll take care of him up there." What more can I say? He was a great guy.

I watched the EMTs put Daniel in the ambulance and watched the ambulance pull out. "Are you OK?" asked the policeman who had stayed with me during this time. "Do you want me to follow you up to the hospital?" *God, no*, I thought. *The last thing I need is a police escort.* I knew the hospital that the policeman mentioned. It was, in fact, one of the hospitals we had gone to trying to find help. Twice. I assured him that I could find my way there.

"The officer who took his wallet has already left, but I'll stop at the station, get his wallet for you and meet you in the emergency room. That way I'll save you a trip to the police station." I looked at him gratefully, although at that point I had been in my car for about four hours, so another half-hour here or there didn't seem to matter much.

Daniel spent the night in the hospital and I had the best sleep I'd had in months. In the morning, they pronounced him fit as a fiddle and called me to pick him up. I could not believe it. I went to the hospital in the morning and instead of trying to find Daniel, I asked to talk with the nurse in charge.

"My son needs help," I began without introduction. "He doesn't need a ride home. He was on some kind of drug yesterday, don't you realize that? You can't possibly think that a good night's sleep is all he needed. How can you possibly think that sending him home with me is any kind of solution?"

"I'm sorry, but your son's not a minor and I'm not allowed to discuss his medical history with you."

"He was completely incoherent when he arrived here last night. He was under the influence of some crazy combination of drugs. You and I both know it. I don't want to discuss his medical history, I want you to help me. Don't you have a detox unit here at the hospital?" I asked. "Isn't it possible to transfer him to that unit?"

"We *did* have a detox unit," she answered, "not anymore. Closed down a few months ago, but I can help you." She picked up a piece of paper, wrote a few words and a phone number on it and passed it over to me. "This is the only detox unit left in our area. You can talk to them." I looked at the piece of paper and recognized the name of the hospital that Daniel had been turned away from on several different occasions. Another dead end.

"Good luck to you," she said sweetly.

I went to find Daniel, who was already dressed and raring to go. "I need to get home and get my suboxone," he said.

"This has got to stop, Daniel."

"I know, I know. I'm really sorry. I don't know how it happened."

"Why don't we try again at the hospital?" I showed him the paper the nurse had given me.

"I'm tired, Mom. I really am. Maybe tomorrow."

During this time, I read about a minister who had set up a non-denominational church in what was apparently the hub of drugs and crime in one of the local cities. I found the address on the internet, realized that it was not far from where my car accident had occurred and went there one Sunday morning. The service was held not in any traditional church but rather in a drab brick building, not much different from the buildings that surrounded it. But when I got inside, I found it was bustling with activity. There was a line to get into the main room where the service was held, and once I entered, I was amazed to find it packed with people of all ages and attire.

There didn't seem to be any seats available and so I stood by the door and listened to the opening music played by a six-piece rock band. Eventually an usher noticed me and offered me his seat. The minister came on stage after the band cleared off their instruments and he was nothing short of dynamic.

"How many of you have ever been in jail?" he shouted out to the congregation at one point. I found myself surrounded by a sea of hands. "Well, let me tell you, you are still in jail, still in captivity unless you turn your life over to God and let him free you."

"Amen," everyone responded.

The churches I was used to had tall stained-glass windows and cushioned pews, organ music and rows and rows of empty seats, except on Christmas Eve. Here we sat on folding metal chairs crammed one against the other and instead of stained glass windows, there were two large screens that broadcast Bible verses and words to songs and occasionally scenic nature photos. It would have been impossible to fall asleep in this church. People waved their arms and shouted out "amens", occasionally hugged the person next to them and actually *danced* to some of the music that was played. Not my kind of service, but at the same time, I had to admit that something important was going on in that church that day.

At the end of the service, the minister invited anyone who wanted prayer, or alternatively, if anyone who wanted to *stand in* for anyone needing prayer, to come forward. I was puzzled by this. *Stand in for someone else?* I had never heard of that before, but I found the idea intriguing.

A few people got up to leave, but there were many more who wandered up to the stage to stand in line for a prayer. I waited until the lines thinned out and then stood at the end of one of them. When it was finally my turn, I looked at the man who was facing me and said simply: "My son is a heroin addict. I want to stand in for him."

"OK," he responded, "but I'd like to pray for you too." I immediately panicked. "Don't worry about me," I assured him. "Let's just focus on him." Good god, I didn't want the prayer *diluted* by splitting it between two people. And so he prayed for Daniel. And then he prayed for me too, the loveliest, kindest prayer I think I have ever heard. I felt tears welling up in my eyes as he prayed, and I cried all the way to my car that day, I'm not sure why.

Of course, if I had gone back to that church years later and heard that same question again, I could have raised my hand along with everyone else. Not that I myself had been incarcerated, but Daniel had been and I had been to visit there, a unique experience in itself. By that time Daniel was in a program with strict rules; he had not committed any kind of crime, but he had broken one of the rules of the program and that was enough to land him in jail.

Visiting someone in jail is a very humbling experience. First of all, there is a dress code, dictated by the fact that any piece of metal however small—a zipper, a snap, the tiny screw in a set of plastic eye glasses, for God's sake—is enough to set off the metal detector and bar your entry, and you quickly discover that virtually everything you own has metal somewhere. Jim managed to look fairly respectable, but the best I could come up with was an oversized pair of sweat pants, fitness bra (no metal clasp!), un-matching t-shirt and bedroom slippers. I would have felt more comfortable dressed in a Halloween costume. I also learned that there was a certain routine that everyone follows mindlessly: you pass your license through a slot and get a key which opens a locker where you can store everything you have forgotten to lock up in your car. As you wait, you carefully note who has come before and after you so when the buzzer sounds, you know where to place yourself in the entry line. It is not Southwest Airlines, after all. You're on your own here. Being first in line has its benefits of course because you get first choice of the cubicles inside, the first and last being the most preferable because they give at least the illusion of privacy.

Once the whole group has passed through the metal detector, the main door opens electronically and you choose your cubicle. It is hard to imagine what color the cubicles were originally painted, but now they are the color of old guacamole. The pungent smell of dirty stale air is everywhere. You get a few minutes to settle into your cubicle on the little metal stool fastened to the floor before the inmates arrive. Jim and I always seemed to find ourselves in the third cubicle, distinguished by the fact that someone had etched into the paint "Marvin was here." *Marvin and I and how many others?* And you wait hesitantly, not knowing what awaits you on the other side of the plexiglass window—frustration, despair or sheer boredom? Though the cubicles seem to indicate some degree of privacy, in fact there is none. You can hear everything being said on both sides, not that it matters much, because everyone seems to be saying the same thing: hang in there, everything is fine at home, we miss you, you'll be out in no time. And when the buzzer signaling the end of the visit comes, there is a poignant moment when each of us instinctively puts our palm up against the plexiglass window to meet the palm of the person on the other side, hoping that this says everything that didn't get said during the visit.

I know that there are people who think that jail is the answer to addiction, but there is a little-known fact that merits some consideration: drugs flow more freely than water in some jails. You may not be able to sneak in with a metal clip on your bra, but drugs seem to find their way in there. How they get in is anyone's guess.

Meanwhile juggling work and home life was a constant battle. Half of the time I arrived to work exhausted before I even walked in the door and turned on my computer. Quitting my job was not an option either because money had become a pressing need. At one point, I lost a job and found another one at just a fraction of my previous salary. Bills were piling up, and our credit plummeted to the point that we wouldn't have been able to get a loan, even if we tried. I made a point of not telling Daniel where I was working, made a point of never calling him from the office phone. Throughout the day, he would call Jim's and my cell phone and leave desperate messages: "Pick up. Call me back, call me back as soon as you get this message. It's really important this time." Inevitably the calls were all about money. Leaving the house peacefully was close to impossible. At times Daniel would literally barricade the door or stand behind our car so we couldn't leave without running over him.

As crazy as it sounds, Jim and I would actually try to plan out who would leave first in the morning—in other words, who would get the chance to escape and who would be left to deal with Daniel. And now and then these plans would work; other times both of us would get caught up in the morning chaos; still other times, one of us would simply sacrifice the other just to escape the house.

One morning I discovered that Jim had left for work before me, and I was there with Daniel and no spare money. I panicked because I knew where this was headed. I couldn't miss work again, I couldn't even afford to be late again. Daniel had heard Jim leave and he came downstairs immediately. We were like two caged animals, carefully keeping an eye on one another. He was closely watching the front door and I was nervously watching the clock, calculating my next move. The phone rang and as he went to answer it, I seized the moment. I was still in bedroom slippers, but I quickly grabbed a pair of boots and a jacket on the way and darted out the back door. There was a foot of un-shoveled snow I needed to get through on my way to the car and there was a biting rain of sleet outside, but I was determined to escape. I clumsily made my way across the yard, and although I could hear him clomping through the snow behind, I thought for a moment I was going to make it. *Home free. Free from home.* But then unexpectedly, just yards away from my car, I hit an icy patch of snow and fell. My boots scattered and in a second Daniel was beside me kneeling in the snow. "My, God, Mom," he said, "what are you doing?" We locked eyes for one minute and we both knew there was no need to answer that question. *I am a mother desperately trying to escape my own son.* He sighed, picked up my scattered boots and reached down to help me up. "My God, Mom," he said simply. "What has happened to us?"

One time just before Christmas I had an important meeting I needed to attend. I didn't want to take the risk of being delayed by heated arguments, flying objects, overturned furniture and produce some lame excuse for why I was arriving late once again. So I got up in the middle of the night, grabbed a toothbrush, dressed for work and drove to the rest stop on the thruway mid-way between home and the next day's meeting. I expected to be the only car in the parking area at that time of the night, but to my surprise, there were a couple of other cars there with drivers already asleep at the wheel. *What are they doing here*? I wondered. I wasn't planning to spend the night with a group of strangers, but there didn't seem to be any alternative at that point. I settled into a parking place under the bright overhead lights, locked my car door, set my phone alarm, pushed back my seat and was about to shut off the car when a familiar Christmas carol came over the radio: *Silent Night, Holy Night, all is calm. All is bright....* *Sleep in heavenly peace, sleep in heavenly peace.* And I did. I woke up to my phone alarm refreshed and energized and realized that for the first time in weeks I was about to arrive to work on time.

I AM A ROCK, I AM AN ISLAND

hile Daniel could stand mid-deep in snow and ask "What has happened to us?" this was not a question I ever asked myself. I *knew* what we had become. We had become the family that no one wants their kid to associate with, the family no one invites to neighborhood parties. When the police cruiser came down the block, no one wondered which house they would be going to— they all knew. And what they didn't know, I am sure the neighbors suspected. Strange cars parked in the driveway in the middle of the day when we were at work, strange people going in and out of the house, a window boarded up here and there, broken furniture left on the curb for the garbage men to pick up.

At the beginning when we thought this was just a temporary situation that would soon be solved, Jim and I would vent our frustrations, try to reach out to each other, talk about solutions. We would use expressions like "When this is all over...." But as the years rolled by with no solution in sight, we stopped looking to each other for support. We were so consumed by our own pain and frustration, there just didn't seem to be enough room to shoulder someone else's. During this time, our dog died too. She was old, she was sick, we should have somehow prepared ourselves for this, but we hadn't. She had been a faithful companion to all of us for fifteen years, so this loss just made the landscape at home seem even more bleak.

What had happened to us? We had become the classic dysfunctional family, living in chaos, wary of each other, resentful toward each other for not making it all stop! distanced from each other because of the sheer enormity of trying to keep our own heads above water. The most routine of tasks—getting to work, going to school, paying bills, even mowing the lawn—became major accomplishments. We were little islands, each in our own worlds, each struggling with our own thoughts, concerns and emotions.

Over time, we lost contact with almost all friends and relatives, stopped meeting with colleagues after work. What in the world could we talk about? We didn't go on exciting vacations, read the most current books, watch movies or follow any television series. A simple question like "What are you up to these days?" or "How are you?" would leave me speechless. Was it better to lie with the simple response, "Fine, fine," and quickly change the subject or try to share the horrors of a world that even you cannot make sense of? For the most part, we chose the first option.

Immersed in our own problems, we lost track of other people's birthdays and anniversaries and didn't bother with things so simple as sending out Christmas cards. One year I didn't even bother to open the few Christmas cards we received—I knew each would contain a cheerful letter with yearly updates and photos. I didn't want to read news about other people's children finishing college, going on semesters abroad, building their careers. I didn't want to see pictures of family vacations, graduations, weddings. I didn't want to read any "Joy to the World" messages from anyone. In fact, I didn't want any messages at all from anyone. I was in my own cocoon, and things outside of my cocoon just didn't seem relevant.

My husband's family literally lived on another continent entirely, and although my family lived close by, a rift had developed between us and the extended family. Things had gone missing and the blame was placed squarely on Daniel. They had been hurt and their response was to shut their doors. I don't blame them, maybe if the situation had been reversed, I might have done the same, but it certainly didn't help my situation. Holidays from that point on were celebrated, if you can even use that word, in two places—my parents' house and ours. Year after year, with aging parents and as the only daughter, I helped make Thanksgiving dinner at my parents' house, ate there with a group of relatives who ignored, resented, maybe in some cases even hated my son and brought home leftovers to eat with Daniel who had spent the day alone or with "friends". It was a HORRIBLE solution, I'm the first to admit it, but there didn't seem to be any better alternative. The four of us could hardly have spent a happy holiday together at home, and bringing Daniel with us would have created such an atmosphere of tension that the day would be ruined for everyone. What would be the point?

Though I have no happy memories of Thanksgiving Day during those years, it just seemed a way to preserve some semblance of happiness, some sense of *family* for everyone else. Tradition, routine...the glue of every family. We never actually talked about Daniel's absence; no one ever asked where he was or how he was doing, and I never talked about how agonizing it felt for me to have my family torn apart every holiday. But apparently it did not go completely unnoticed. To her credit, one year my mother announced to the family that she was not going to go through another Thanksgiving without Daniel at the table. Although she was in her nineties at the time, she was not one to mince words. What she actually said was this: "I am sick of this! You all sit around as if you've never done anything wrong in your life. Let me tell you this: If Daniel is not at the table next Thanksgiving, I won't be there either. And if any of you don't like it, you don't have to be there either." She had been raised in an immigrant family, orphaned at a young age and knew what it was like to face tough times. She also knew more about forgiveness than anyone else who sat at the table. She died before that next Thanksgiving at the ripe old age of 92, but I will forever sing her praises for that comment.

Tell people that your child has cancer, has been in an accident, has a serious disability and they will flock to your side ready to provide support, encouragement, assistance. They will make meals, start fund-raisers, send cheerful notes and emails just to show they *care*. Tell them your child has an addiction, and they all move away and make a point of keeping a safe distance. The shame of it all! Moreover, it is not a disclosure that slips easily into any conversation.

"Oh, my son just graduated from Stanford and plans to start on a Master's degree in the fall," someone will say. "What's Daniel up to these days?"

"Oh, well, he's graduated from heroin to an alternative drug, attends group counseling for addiction regularly and hopes to get off probation within the year."

You see, the easy flow of conversation stops right there. Addiction makes people feel *uncomfortable*. It somehow fits into the category with income tax evasion and extramarital affairs—things that don't need to be shared with other people.

Because of this awkwardness, I was particularly grateful for the few friends who knew about the situation at home, who didn't mind if I forgot their birthdays, drank more than my share of the wine or stopped inviting them to the house. There wasn't much they could do to help other than be there on the sidelines, but it is always good to know you have someone rooting for you, especially when you seem to be losing the game.

The question that plagued me during those years was not "What *has* happened to us?' but rather "What *will* happen to us?" I was forever cognizant of the fact that it could all end badly. But even within the category of bad endings, there were many possibilities. I may have been cut off from many social and family ties, but I was not completely cut off from the world. I read of overdoses, of drug-related crimes, of suicides, of shootings. I knew that more than 40,000 people died yearly from overdoses, and the lives of thousands more were train-wrecked by drugs. I knew that addiction was a dark and dangerous world and full recovery was an elusive goal. I no longer had the confidence that we were all going to make it through this whole experience unscathed or even alive for that matter. I struggled to picture a happy ending to this, a silver lining to a dark cloud and could come up with nothing. In fact, I spent countless hours sitting in an Adirondack chair staring into nothingness—the "abyss" I called it—just wondering about where we were all headed.

We all tried to make a go of it, to keep some semblance of our old relationships. Occasionally Daniel would help Jim fix things at the house or offer to clean up after dinner. Now and then he would share a funny video he'd found online and we would spend a pleasant moment together, but then the chaos would begin all over again. He needed money, he needed a ride, he needed more suboxone and the intensity of his cravings would erupt into intimidation and aggression. Later, Daniel would offer apologies, he would try to make amends. Part of this may have been manipulation, but I truly believe another part of it was that he was genuinely sorry for what was happening, and he himself didn't know how to make it stop.

As frustrating as he could be at times, it was hard not to pity him. He seemed to be deteriorating before our very eyes: the sparkle in his eyes had dimmed, he rarely smiled, he seemed to take no interest whatsoever in the way he dressed. There were times when I saw him on the street and hardly recognized him.

As for the rest of us, we seemed to be just treading water and not doing such a great job of that either. Over time I had lost all interest in mending broken things—I did without, I hung pictures over dents in the wall, I replaced things with tag sale purchases with no regard whatsoever to aesthetics. At one time a person filled with energy, new projects, bold ideas and initiatives, I was now a person who filled her time with meaningless activities—knitting scarves, doing crossword puzzles, doodling—things that would fill the time yet not take my attention away from the situation at hand. I wanted to stay on constant alert, afraid to be caught off guard, as if staying alert was my talisman for warding off evil, protecting me from the inevitable, whatever that might be.

Like good soldiers, we did our best to help Daniel follow routines—group sessions, individual sessions, appointments with the probation department, appointments with doctors, appointments at court. It seemed to go on eternally. Rats in a maze, always running into obstacles, taking wrong turns, ever scurrying onward but with no end in sight. Twiddling my life away sitting in a car or staring into a blank future seemed to be the new normal for me.

I was tired of trying to find a way into some kind of meaningful treatment for Daniel; I was tired of being on the treadmill of counseling. How long did we have to keep doing the same thing over and over before someone realized that it just wasn't working? What I wanted was help, not talk.

One day, Daniel and I were supposed to meet with his lawyer at court in a nearby city. We arrived with time to spare, but there were no parking places to be found anywhere in the vicinity of the court. Finally I let Daniel out in front of the courthouse to meet with the lawyer, while I continued to circle the streets looking for a parking lot or an open space somewhere. On my third time around the block of the courthouse, a man stepped into the street and motioned for me to stop. I paused and rolled down the window.

"You need a place to park?" he asked. Apparently, he had been watching me the whole time. "I have that blue truck over there," he said, gesturing to a designated parking area next to an apartment complex. "I'm on my way to work so you're welcome to use my spot all day if you want. I'll pull out and you can pull in."

That's my idea of help—being offered the thing you need at the time you need it, without having to beg for it, deserve it or bare your soul to get it.

As bleak as our life often seemed, there were isolated moments during those years, moments when Daniel was *willing* to try an inpatient setting and detox. Not *determined*, not *committed* to the idea, but at least *willing* to give it a try. These were moments that prompted us to action. Jim and I would encourage Daniel, commend him on his decision and then try to seize the opportunity: we would make phone calls, drive to a hospital, contact rehab centers, try any avenue available to get him a bed, but it never seemed to work out. There were always hoops to jump through and in the process of going through hoops, the courage to try inpatient would wane. Daniel and the whole treatment system were hopelessly out of sync with one another.

I talked a lot with God in those days. Frustrated as I was, I still believed that He could change the situation, was in fact *willing* to change the situation and yet I didn't get any clear sense of guidance or any vision of how this might happen. I reminded Him of miracles He had done in the past and pointed out how petty my situation was in comparison. I was even bold enough to quote scripture to him: *If he shall ask an egg, will he offer him a scorpion? If he ask a fish, will he give him a serpent?* What about that? When I wanted to adopt a child, I didn't think I was going to be handed this bundle of trouble.

And above all, I felt God's timing was way off. This whole thing had gone on far too long. I didn't want an extra dosage of patience, I wanted deliverance for my son and I wanted it *now*. If this whole experience was going to make us all better people somehow, we were paying an awfully high price for personal improvement. I pointed out that our little Humpty Dumpty family was already so broken that possibly no one, not all the king's horses and all the king's men, not even He, would be able to piece us back together again.

One day when I sitting in the living room, Travis came downstairs, bag in hand. He was a full teenager now, tall, self-assured. He put the bag down and without introduction said simply, "Just wanted to tell you that I'm leaving."

"For the weekend? Where are you going?"

"Not just for the weekend. I am leaving. Really leaving. I don't want to live here anymore."

His words fell with a thud. I don't know how long we stayed there looking at each other, but it seemed to go on forever. In the duration of those minutes, a thousand thoughts flashed through my head. Travis was fed up with Daniel, blamed him for destroying our family, resented the fact that he had become the focus of family attention. I thought of the story of the prodigal son, specifically the bitterness of the stay-at-home brother who had done everything right and yet never reaped the rewards that his brother did. I realized that what Travis was silently demanding was nothing more than an ordinary peaceful home life, and he had given up hope. Who could blame him for that? He had tried everything he knew to make it work; he had lost faith in us, in himself. If he couldn't save us, he wanted to save himself. Was that so unreasonable?

On the one hand, he was abandoning us; on the other hand, I knew there was a part of him that was solidly loyal to Jim and me. I dreaded the day that in trying to protect us, he and Daniel would get in a fight whose outcome would bring devastation to all of us. I don't know why, but Cain and Abel flashed through my mind.

"So…who are you going to stay with?" I asked. "Do I know them?"

He practically laughed. "Really?" he said. "Why should you care? You're worried about me staying in a normal household? After living here, normal is going to feel like a vacation. Did you forget what normal looks like? Normal people make popcorn and watch television and order in pizza on Friday nights. Is that good enough for you? Normal people don't have fits of rage and turn over furniture and punch holes in walls. They care about each other." He hesitated. "And, you know, these people care about me."

"Heh, I care about you too," I said. He said nothing.

What did he want from me? To beg him to stay in a toxic environment, a house that was unhealthy, dark and dangerous? Was he asking for my blessing on his decision or did he just want to hurt me for not doing a better job of protecting him, of preserving the family, of solving the problem? I didn't know. What I did know was that on one level, he was as scared of the prospect of moving out as I was. He was not scared of being on his own—he had learned to be independent years before; he was scared about what might happen if he were not there. We could have talked longer, I could have tried to persuade him to give it one more try, but there was no point. Instinctively I knew at this moment in our lives, there was no other option: the only way to protect him was to let him go.

"This is only temporary," I said. "This is your home, we love you…even if you don't believe that right now."

He picked up his suitcase. End of conversation. "Someone is picking me up," he said. "I see the lights outside." He hesitated when he got to the door and looked back at me. "Call me if you need me," he said and then he opened the door.

"I'll call you every day," I responded, "whether I need you or not."

And without a glance backward, he left. From the window, I watched him put his suitcase in the car, watched him get into the front seat, watched the car swing around and watched until the lights disappeared into the night. And for the first time in a very, very long time, I just sat on the sofa and cried. I cried for Travis, I cried for our lost dog, I cried because I mourned the loss of the life we had once had, a life which I doubted we would ever have again.

The Pit and the Pendulum

Through the years, I often pondered the question that had been posed to me on that first day of phone calls: *Does he want help?* I could never come up with a clear answer to that question, or rather the answer fluctuated from day to day. Daniel rarely fought going to any of the multiple appointments at addiction counseling centers. In fact, there were times when he seemed to *enjoy* group sessions. On the ride home, he would talk enthusiastically about the people he met, the comments they made, the movies he saw. That said to me that he wanted help; yet there were other times when it seemed as if he sabotaged any effort to get help. He made appointments on his own to meet with a counselor, but later he would cancel or find some reason to re-schedule. I would drop him off at the building and find out later that he just sat in the lobby and never went in for his appointment. He voluntarily packed a suitcase on a couple of occasions when it seemed as if there might be a bed available in a residential treatment facility, but didn't seem particularly disappointed when it didn't work out and we loaded the suitcase back into the car. One time when I picked up his suitcase, I discovered that it was empty and realized he never had any intention of going into the facility; he just wanted to temporarily appease me. He would spend hours trying to get an appointment with a suboxone doctor, but once he had one, it wasn't long before he would do something that would get himself terminated with the doctor.

Did he really want help? The answer was, of course, yes or no, depending on the day or his mood. A couple of times he and another friend with an addiction actually drove to a hospital which offered a three-day detox program. A quick fix, like a car wash or something. They didn't get in, supposedly because they didn't have severe enough symptoms. So according to Daniel they went out, smoked a little weed and then instead of going back, they decided that it wasn't such a good idea after all. Daniel was afraid of detox; he admitted as much himself. Somewhere he had heard of someone who had died in detox. "Really?" I would say sarcastically whenever he brought this up. "What about all the people who die of overdoses? On the other hand, what about the thousands of people who have survived detox and gone on to lead successful lives?"

"I'm not taking the risk of dying in detox," he would say emphatically. End of story. So in the meantime, he was just destroying himself little by little. Don't take chances—go for the surefire thing. What a great plan.

The other question that nagged at me was *How long is this going to go on?* or rather the flip side *How much longer can we hang on?*

Because we wavered too. We were treading water—financially, emotionally, physically. There were moments when things spiraled so out of control that it seemed as if we would all be sucked under.

And there was a daunting question that loomed over us: How do we determine the moment that we stop trying to save him and instead try to save ourselves??

At first, we were waiting for to Daniel to hit bottom. That was apparently the point at which things changed. But it seemed he hit bottom, we hit bottom, time and time again and nothing ever seemed to change. Certainly, he reached points where he was overcome with hopelessness, moments that were not about money or drugs, but moments that would send an ice cold chill up my back. "I'm done," he'd say. "I know I will never escape this. It will *never* get any better. There's no point in even trying to go on. I may as well just end it." And I would wonder if this is the feeling that overtakes people who throw themselves in front of cars and off bridges, if this was attitude of people who blindly take any drug offered to them, no questions asked. *Never* is a cold bleak word, devoid of any hope. Somehow this feeling of despair, of reckless abandonment, scared me even more than the drugs.

And I began to seriously question whether in fact there was a bottom or whether the whole idea was completely bogus. After all, there were thousands of people Daniel's age who were dying before they ever had a chance to reach the top or the bottom either. Maybe instead of a bottom, there was just this bottomless pit that we swung back and forth over until one of us got tired enough or impulsive enough to let go and drop in. Somewhere I read that the bottom is nothing more than the moment you experience just prior to the moment that you decide to change. Now that sure is a moving target if I ever heard of one.

We finally reached the point where we felt we had to get Daniel out of our house, not out of our lives but out of our house. We needed to reclaim our own sanity, our own house, our own lives. I had two sons, after all, and it bothered me no end that one was not at home. Sure, Travis and I talked by phone, we met now and then, he came for Thanksgiving dinner at my parents' house, but he wanted no part of coming home.

"What about Christmas?" I asked him as December rolled around. "You'll be here for Christmas, won't you? You'll come and help me decorate the tree, won't you? I'll arrange a time when Daniel isn't at home."

"Don't you understand, Mom? I don't want to go into our house… too many bad memories there."

"Suppose we meet somewhere else? We can go out to dinner together, meet at someone else's house."

"Sure, whatever."

But when we met outside the restaurant we'd chosen, neither of us felt any urge to go in. We sat in the car, talked, watched happy families and couples go in and out of the restaurant, listened to faint sounds of Christmas music coming from inside.

"I'm not really all that hungry," he finally said.

"You know, neither am I." The truth is, we didn't seem to fit in with the festive spirit.

"How are you? I mean really."

"I am fine, Mom, I really am. Don't worry about me. How are things at home?"

"Well, your brother is back in counseling...."

"In other words, nothing has changed."

I would have liked to say, "Not now, but things will change soon. This is all going to end soon, I promise you," but I didn't have the heart to say something I didn't even believe myself. We exchanged Christmas gifts that year in the back seat of my car.

Daniel announced early on that he didn't want presents that year, money would be just fine. *Surprise. Surprise.* This put somewhat of a damper on the whole celebration. He had always loved all the "hoopdela" of Christmas, from stringing the outside lights, to snitching the holiday cookies, placing his favorite ornaments on the tree, even going to candlelight service on Christmas Eve, but he seemed indifferent to it all now. Jim and I tried to muster up a little enthusiasm for the holiday by putting up a tree and bringing a few boxes of decorations down from the attic, but by Christmas Eve the tree was still untrimmed, the decorations still in the boxes.

"Let's at least go to candlelight service," said Jim. "We can decorate the tree when we get back." To our surprise, a few minutes before we left for the candlelight service, Daniel came downstairs and announced that he wanted to go with us. *Was there some ulterior motive for wanting to get in the car with us?* I wondered, but I simply said, "Grab your coat. Maybe this year we'll actually arrive on time."

It ended up being the only family tradition we kept that year. Inside the church a dozen Christmas Eves collapsed into one. "*For unto you is born this day in the city of David....*" I remembered the year that Daniel and Travis wore crisp white robes and tinsel halos as angels in the Christmas pageant, another year that Daniel had actually stood in front and proudly read part of the scripture. When the time came, the three of us instinctively tipped our candles to light each other's and held them out in front of us. I listened to Jim and Daniel sing out the final stanzas of *Silent Night*, their faces aglow in the candlelight and realized that for one moment, the sadness of our lives was briefly suspended, and we let ourselves believe there was still peace, maybe even hope, for us somewhere down the line.

The problem in helping Daniel move onto a more independent life was that he had no money, no offers to share an apartment. We had no money to put him up in an apartment, and I truly doubted whether he could survive on his own anyway. He just barely functioned living under our roof. We actually reached the point one night that we drove Daniel to a homeless shelter where there was a neon sign that announced in chartreuse letters: *Jesus Saves.* I know it sounds like a detail from a novel, but it is actually true. With no end in sight, we were at a breaking point. We couldn't go on any longer without some kind of change.

There was a parking lot in front of the shelter and we pulled in. Daniel made no attempt to get out. "We can't live like this anymore," I said simply. "Something has to change."

Jim got out, opened the rear door of the car and waited. Daniel didn't budge. "I'm not getting out," he said. "I'm not going to be homeless."

Wrong answer. What I was hoping for was some kind of commitment, some willingness to steer his life in a different direction. It didn't happen. It just wasn't there.

We stayed there in the dark empty parking lot across from the homeless shelter for some time, with back and forth comments that seemed to lead nowhere. We might have gone on all night like this had it not been for an elderly unshaven man in a shabby oversized coat who suddenly appeared at our side.

"Got some change, Mister? Got any spare change? I just need enough to get a little food and a coffee down the street." He stood there waiting. "Haven't had anything to eat all day."

We locked eyes with the man for a few minutes, and then Jim instinctively felt in his pockets for money.

"You have anything you could give him?" he asked. I searched through my pocketbook and managed to come up with a couple of dollars and a few coins. *Change, change, we're all looking for change.*

At that point Daniel joined in. "Hey, bud," he called out. "Can't you see we're trying to have some family time here?"

"Oh, oh, sorry," he said sheepishly, and he backed away as if he had unwittingly stumbled onto a Hallmark moment. Jim held out the money, he took it and then he was gone. *Quality time as a family. Right.*

And that was it for me. I'm not sure why, but the whole thing struck me as so enormously ridiculous that I just couldn't muster up the energy to keep it going. Jim eventually got back in the car, started the engine and we drove off. Along the way, we passed the man from the parking lot climbing the steps into the local liquor store.

Another time I went to the police station to look into the procedure for evicting someone from the house. It doesn't happen overnight, you know, the officer said. You first have to serve notice…and he went on. It was basically the same as trying to evict someone from an apartment. Hopeless, or at least not the solution we needed. But we needed to do *something*, something that would somehow change the direction in which we were heading. So we toyed with the idea of going to court.

"I'm not on board with a restraining order," Jim said from the start. "I don't think we can just cut him loose like that, and besides, I don't think a piece of paper is going to stop him from doing what he wants to do anyway." But I later found out there was something called a refrain order, an order that says, in essence, you better not step too far over the line, because Big Brother, the court system will be watching. I found someone to help me write up a petition and I went alone to court, expecting that this would be a smooth process. However, when I appeared in front of the judge, he said he didn't want to grant me a refrain order; he wanted to give me a restraining order. This would mean, of course, that there could be no contact whatsoever with Daniel or there would be police intervention.

Could Daniel survive on his own in his current condition? I seriously doubted it. Would he violate a restraining order and show up at our house? In a heartbeat…and that would generate just one more complication with the law. A restraining order would essentially put Daniel out on the street with no resources whatsoever. He could not have found or kept a job. He had no reliable friends he could move in with or who could help him if he needed it. A resourceful person might be able to find a way to survive on the streets, but Daniel was anything but resourceful at that point. It is one thing to allow someone to tread water on their own; it is another to desert a person who you know cannot swim, or worse yet, be the hand the pushes him under.

It's amazing how personal standards and guidelines seem to erode when you live in the same household as an addict. However, there is one guideline that Jim and I had clung to throughout the years: whatever decisions had to be made, wherever this path would lead us, whatever the outcome, he and I would stand together. We couldn't afford to be split in two directions. It was one guideline that I wasn't ready to give up. Stand by me, as the song goes...come what may.

I am not sure how much time lapsed as we all sat there in silence in the courtroom, but it felt as if it were hours. I longed desperately for something that might turn our lives around, and yet I dreaded making a move that would send us headlong into even greater chaos. I looked up at the ceiling with its elaborate carved design and thought simply this: *If this is the direction I am supposed to take, I need a crystal-clear answer.* I listened for a still, small voice in the deep silence of the room, but there was none.

Finally I looked straight at the judge. "With all due respect," I said, "I can't go along with a restraining order at this time. If you can't grant me a refrain order, then I guess I'll just have to leave here empty-handed. My apologies for taking up your time."

I gathered my coat and purse and was about to leave on that note, but in the end, the judge relented and granted a refrain order which meant if there were trouble on home territory, that trouble would spill into the courts. And it meant that one day a month, we were expected to take an hour-long ride to the courthouse and appear before another judge who would cheerfully ask Daniel and me, "And how are we doing?"

He was a nice man, he seemed genuinely interested in us, and we did our best to engage in meaningful conversation with him. Actually, home life was improving in some small ways, and we made sure to point this out. The judge never asked us about drugs and we didn't bring up the topic either. Neither of us wanted to open a can of worms in a court setting: Daniel certainly didn't want any more trouble in his life, and I was missing work more often than I could afford to with these monthly visits. This did nothing to solve Daniel's addiction, but it did have its benefits after all; it set a good tone for the conversation on the ride home and made us feel somehow that we were both on the same team. I recognize that going to court to get a refrain order against your own son who lives in the same house as you is more than just another erosion of norms; it is downright *bizarre*, but, on the other hand, it did keep the lid on things for a while.

The fact is, I never lost sight of the fact that I had a life with Daniel for seventeen years before he started using alcohol and drugs. There were years when we happily swung our skis onto the rung of the chair lift and spent the ride chattering about the snow and the view and how many runs we would take before we met up in the lodge for hot chocolate. Years when we rode bikes along country roads and took hikes and make brownies together. Years when he was the official turkey baster at Thanksgiving and the first one awake on Christmas morning ready to take down the stockings. There were lobster dinners and trips to the beach, talks around the fireplace, cub scout meetings and soccer games. And while things had changed enormously, there were still times when I had a glimpse of that same child, when for one reason or another, there was a suspension of time and place and we would slip back into NORMAL, a reality that had once been our everyday life. Those years and those moments carried enough weight to keep the pendulum swinging and keep me hanging on.

And, of course, there was one experience that was the most vivid of them all, and that was the day we first met.

After what seemed to be endless paperwork, interviews and assessments, we had been put on the list to adopt a baby and informed at the same time that it would likely be years before we were ever contacted. Not exactly an encouraging message: the good news is that you are on our list; the bad news is that we may never get to you. Life went on and for the most part, we forgot that we were creeping up on a list somewhere beyond our everyday world. But one night I received a phone call just before midnight. It was from the adoption agency.

"We have a baby available for adoption, but you have to give me an answer now," the voice said. "It's already late and I want to get this taken care of tonight, so if you're not interested, let me know and I'll just call the next name on the list."

What??

Jim wasn't even at home at the time. We hadn't talked about, even thought about, adoption for months. Our last contact with the adoption agency had been six months before, and I didn't even remember finishing up the paperwork for them. We didn't own as much as a stick of baby furniture or a baby bottle. I took a moment to catch my breath and then asked: "When would this take place?"

"If you're really going to go through with this, you need to be on the plane tomorrow morning." Although I was half asleep when I picked up the phone, I was definitely awake now. *Tomorrow morning?* She paused, sighed heavily, and then said, "Well, I need to know. What's it going to be?"

I begged her for five minutes to at least call Jim before answering. He was as astonished as I was but definitely on board with moving ahead.

I called the woman back and listened to the phone ring and ring. *Pick up, pick up!* I called out to her mentally and eventually she did. "OK, we'll be there tomorrow," I said confidently although I hadn't even called the airline yet. Luckily, I was able to get a reservation for the next morning and was about to wake up my boss to let him know I would be missing from work for a while when it occurred to me that our lives were about to take a major turn with no other information than this: it's a boy, he's one-month old and he appears to be healthy.

We took the first flight out so we didn't have time to do anything more than throw a few clothes in a bag. On the plane ride, we tossed names back and forth. We tried to think about names alphabetically, went through family names, went through names of people we knew or had read about. We were still debating between Max and Daniel when the plane touched down. "Let's go with Daniel," Jim said as we picked up our luggage. "You OK with that?"

And I was. We took a taxi to the adoption agency, met the lawyer, talked about paperwork that still needed to be completed. "You want to take a ride and meet him?" the lawyer asked. On the ride, she told us that the baby was staying with a wonderful foster family who just adored him. "They wanted to adopt him," she said, "but the regulations don't allow it."

The baby was asleep when we arrived, but the foster mom went and woke him up and brought him out to us. He was crying at the time, and she began to cry too. Her husband greeted us briefly, sad and puffy eyed, and then disappeared into another room. The foster mom put the baby in my arms and then tried to soothe him as best as she could. He wanted none of it. He wailed as if his life depended on it. I instinctively tried to hand the baby back to the her since she obviously knew heaps more about babies than I did, but the lawyer stopped me. "He's coming with us," she said. "Didn't you know?"

Didn't I know? I was drawing a blank. *Did someone mention that to me? How could I have missed that detail?* I was really drawing a blank on all levels now. The mother was crying, the baby was crying and now I was crying too. More out of fear than happiness, I suppose. I felt like an imperialist army swooping in to tear a child away from its mother.

But apparently the foster parents had already been informed that the baby was going with us. "Wait a minute," the mother said. She disappeared for a moment and then reappeared with a hand crocheted blanket, a plastic bottle and a tin can. "Here," she said, handing the can to Jim. "It's powder, you just need to read the directions. He usually wants to eat every few hours." And she tenderly wrapped the blanket around the baby.

I thanked her heartily. She kissed the sobbing baby, patted both of us on our arms, wished us the best of luck and turned away.

"Wait a minute," I said. "What do you call him?"

"It's not the name on the birth certificate," she said, "but my husband and I have always called him Daniel."

Daniel? I took it as a sign. A good sign.

As it turned out, I needed some kind of sign, because Daniel cried from that point onward. He cried on the car ride, he cried when we got into the hotel room, he cried the whole time Jim was at the store picking up diapers and other supplies. Neither of us had much experience with babies, but we talked to him, sang to him, jostled him, patted him, fed him, diapered him and still he cried.

As the night went on, we passed Daniel back and forth between us and tried to catch a few minutes of sleep. "Do you think a baby can die from crying?" I asked Jim as I passed Daniel to him.

"I don't know anything about babies," he said, "but in one month, he was abandoned by one mother, woken up from sleep and taken from a loving home and a second mother, and then brought to a hotel room with two strangers. Seems a pretty legitimate reason to cry if you ask me."

And at some point, as the night began to pale into day, Daniel stopped crying. At the time, I was lying on the bed, exhausted by the lack of sleep, hoarse from singing every lullaby I could think of. I was starting to doze off but was suddenly jolted awake by the silence in the room. *My God, did he die?* I wondered in a panic. But he was just breathing quietly, sleeping soundly on top of me and it was one of the sweetest moments I have ever experienced. I tried to stay awake as long as I could then, not because sleep had escaped me, but because I didn't want that moment to ever end. It seemed the purest kind of happiness.

However, I knew I would nod off eventually. I slid him over to one side and as he snuggled up to me, I draped my arm around him. *Like a bird covering her nestlings with her wing*, I remember thinking at the time. *A mother bird protecting her young.*

And with this image still emblazoned in my memory, I wavered back and forth, torn by two powerful drives, the drive for self-survival and the drive to nurture and protect. I had grown to hate everything connected with addiction—the needles, the blackened spoons, the tiny translucent bags, the shady characters, the desperate actions, the lies, the cigarette holes, the frustration, the anguish, the uncertainty of it all. More than anything, I wanted to be done with it all, to get rid of the whole affair.

And therein I stumbled upon one more guideline that had not been lost along the way: No matter how much you're tempted, you don't throw the baby out with the dirty bath water. And with that, the pendulum continued to swing.

Didn't Make the Cut...

As good red-blooded Americans, we love the idea of TEAMwork. Corporate teams, medical teams, athletic teams, therapeutic teams. There is no "I" in TEAM. Yaaah! Go, team, go. Apparently, there is no "P" in TEAM either, because parents never seem to be invited to be on the addiction treatment team. I certainly wasn't. Not that I was looking to run the show, but it would have been nice to hear the team's vision and goals, the general rules of the game, maybe even ask questions or give a little background that might have been helpful. A treatment provider spends perhaps as much as one half-hour a week with a client while a parent or family member can spend as much as 40 hours a week with that same person. You would think perhaps there might be something to be gained by a conversation with a family member. I think many providers are convinced that parents are part of the problem, not part of the solution. It is probably in a textbook somewhere, written in bold letters: **Parents are part of the problem.** You know, if you had done the *right* thing in the *first* place, you wouldn't find yourself in this situation. Maybe if we let you on the team, you'll screw it up all over again.

There is a prevalent sense of distrust. They are the PROFESSIONALS after all. What could I possibly offer? The funny thing is that I am a PROFESSIONAL too. As soon as I mention I have an MSW degree, I have credibility. In some cases, I have trumped them on the education scale. Hundreds of hours in the trenches, sitting in courtrooms, checking in with the probation officer, talking to lawyers, knocking on recovery center door in a 40-mile radius, calling all the suboxone doctors within a 50-mile radius and hundreds more hours of conversations with my addicted son while driving him all over the universe and I have nothing to offer? Apparently not. But mention that I have a MSW degree, graduate of a degree program before I even had children, in which I learned almost nothing about substance abuse, addiction or recovery and the door opens. Just a crack, mind you, but it opens. I am one of them.

Many years ago, I went to hear S. E. Hinton speak. You might remember her…the one who wrote *The Outsiders*, a book that captured the imagination of thousands of young readers. Though she talked at length, I remember only one thing from that talk. She mentioned that despite the fact that she is a writer, an avid reader and had read faithfully to her son when he was a child, she had raised a non-reader, or rather she raised a child who was basically uninterested in reading. This captured my attention because it hit upon an often-neglected truth—sometimes you can follow the formula and not get the result you expected. There is no guarantee that if you follow the yellow brick road long enough, you will eventually reach the Land of Oz. Along the way are falling houses and poppy fields, flying monkeys and wicked witches. And even if you get to Oz, you may find the door shut in your face.

Like most parents, Jim and I did due diligence in trying to prevent our children from substance abuse. We talked about it frequently, pointed out newspaper articles about the dangers of substance use, gave stern warnings each time Daniel walked out the door with a set of car keys in his hands. It was not a neglected topic in our house. Moreover, there was nothing in our family lifestyle to promote any kind of substance use: we never had a liquor cabinet in the house, never used prescription or non-prescription drugs, never hosted any kind of drinking parties. We went to both sons' DARE graduations and celebrated their commitment to JUST SAY NO! to drugs and alcohol. In fact, the last thing I said to Daniel the night he got drunk and hit a pedestrian was "Don't you even **think** about drinking and driving!" You see how well that worked.

As time went on, communities began to take notice of the prevalence of drug abuse in their local areas and began to have meetings to discuss the problem. I noticed one being held at a local college and called there for more information. "By the way, who's on the panel?" I asked, and the person on the other end of the phone line rattled off a number of names and titles.

"No parents?" I asked. "No former drug users?"

"No," she replied. "It's a panel of professionals and politicians." There was a moment of silence on the line, as though she knew what I was thinking. "We are trying to raise awareness," she finally said, "not look for solutions."

It was unclear to me why we needed to raise awareness considering the fact that the internet and media had been diligent in informing us of celebrity overdoses and statistics for years, but now that addiction had been declared an epidemic, everyone wanted to get in on it. Did we really think that papering our school communities with posters describing the symptoms of drug use and handing out flyers and workbooks to the kids had somehow stemmed the tide of drug usage?

I didn't go to that meeting, but I did go to the next one that was held a few months later. We watched a lengthy movie on heroin and opiate usage and then the heads of a number of state departments and agencies were given five minutes each to share their views. Most of them used their time to impress us with statistics that highlighted the problem. One however, used his five minutes to describe what he called "Lessons Learned". And do you know what lesson he had learned? Parents are the problem. They are enablers and they don't look for help because they fear the stigma attached to drug use.

Really? Really? Who did you poll to reach that conclusion? I wanted to ask. It conveniently lets doctors, pharmaceutical companies and law enforcement off the hook and excuses the whole field of addiction counseling for the lack of a successful track record.

There was no opportunity for audience response and although I signed up to be on a committee as a parent, not as a professional, I was never invited to participate in any committee meetings. However, I played with the idea of attending the next full group meeting wearing a t-shirt with a scarlet "E" for Enabler emblazoned on my chest and a target printed on the back with the following words below it: **Walk a mile in my shoes before shooting.**

Some months later at another meeting I had the opportunity to ask the question that had nagged at me so long: "Why is it," I asked a panel of professionals, "that parents and other family members are routinely, in fact deliberately, excluded from any kind of treatment discussions of the addict? Why is it that the treatment panels and teams, made up of people who in some cases have never even met the person, are qualified to make decisions and yet people who know that addict, who could potentially offer valuable input regarding him or her, are not included?" The room was quiet for a few minutes. The answer, politely phrased was this: "Quite frankly, we do not see parents as resources." I was stunned. Not resources? They certainly become resources when there is no transportation to mandated meetings and counseling. They sure become the go-to resource when it is time for the addict to leave treatment and there is nowhere for him or her to go, and they are fully expected to step up to the plate when physical tests such as drug screenings are mandated and the person has no insurance, no job, and no extra funds to cover the expense. Where the whole recovery process would just fizzle out for lack of services and funding, it is family members who generally keep the gears oiled and running. Ever wonder why the relapse record is so high? People leave jail or treatment with no resources available, no job on the horizon, no stable place to live, no cash in the bank and a stack of bills that have piled up over the months. What do they do? They fall back into patterns that sustained them in the past. They are UN-enabled, unsupported and become one more statistic on the rate of recidivism.

But there is certainly lip service given to parent participation. Most intake papers for treatment generally have a page for a family member to sign. I signed every paper I came my way. "Yes!" I said. "I would welcome the opportunity to participate in family counseling sessions." In most cases, that signature was the full extent of my involvement. I never received a phone call asking me to come in, never had any "follow up" to that note. And believe me, I was readily available. In most cases, I was sitting in the parking lot outside waiting for the session to end so I could drive Daniel back home.

Jim and I...the self-appointed Designated Drivers for lack of other reliable options. We quickly learned that rehab programs had strict rules around attendance and punctuality. Arrive late, the doors are shut; miss a session and you may find your case is closed and you're out in the cold searching for another program. If there was going to be any continuity in Daniel's program, it seemed that we would have to do our part in getting him there.

At one point we found a rehab center which had sessions outside of work hours and I agreed to drive Daniel three nights a week. And this was not such a bad thing because during those times we would fall into the old pattern of mother-son discourse and there were moments when it all felt familiar, as if we were just taking a ride to go skiing. We had a consistent routine going, but months went by without any visible change. Still the panic over money, still evidence that he was using, still conflicts on the home front. I knew that Daniel had signed the paper which allowed me to talk with his counselor, so one day I called her and suggested that perhaps we should be looking at something a little more intensive—inpatient, for example, detox, a residential program, a half-way house. At that point Daniel had logged in *hundreds* of hours of group and individual counseling. Not that that's all bad, mind you, nothing wrong with a little insight and information gained along the way, but it had led me to the conclusion that he was not going to *talk* his way out of addiction.

She called me the next day to say that she had closed his case and transferred it to another center in a nearby city some twenty miles further away, approximately an hour and a half from where I worked.

He needed to attend five days a week from 10 to 12 in the morning. You thought he needed more intensive, well this is more intensive. *So there. Thanks for your input.*

This was intensive all right; this was insane. I reminded her that Daniel didn't have a driver's license, and there was no public transportation available in rural areas. I reminded her where we lived, where I worked, the fact that it would be impossible for me to maintain a job and still drive Daniel to his sessions. We're having enough problems pulling this off as it is; why up the ante?

Insane though it was, we tried to make it work. I took off another day from work and drove up to the center where Daniel was now a client. Problem was, once we got into the city, we got caught on a one-way street, blocked off by an accident and police cars and arrived ten minutes late. Ten minutes, two hours, it didn't matter. He was barred from the program. Bumped from two programs in two days. We were setting new records.

I think part of the distrust that sometimes exists between parents and professionals is that they view the addict through different lenses. Parents are looking through a wide-angle lens that includes images from the past and expectations for the future while professionals are peering through a zoom lens focused on the present. They see what is in front of them and when they zoom out they see the hundreds of other addicts who have sat in that same chair. The lies, the denial, the deceitfulness, the helplessness, and self-destruction are all too familiar to counselors. The person sitting in front of them has most likely failed on any number of levels and it is their job to get him or her back on track. Their eye is trained to look for symptoms— the highway signs that indicate where the road began, whether the addict is on his way to relapse, whether the addict is on the way to recovery. There is a *plan* in place, a best practice that has been used with dozens of other clients.

Parents, on the other hand, focus on their child's uniqueness. They are suspicious about recipes and formulas and treatment plans. After all, in most cases they've already followed the formula for raising a drug-free child. In fact, they most likely have raised other children who haven't had any problems whatsoever with drugs or alcohol, children for whom the formula worked beautifully. But the formula failed miserably for this one child. So they are suspicious of formulas, of advice that might be appropriate for most situations, but might not fit their own. If things don't work out, the counselor can still go home and have a good night's sleep, and there will be someone else to fill the chair in his or her office in the morning. Parents spend the night tossing and turning and asking why and what more can be done and what does the future hold for all of their family because if there are consequences, they know the impact will ripple far beyond their child. In the morning they will wake up to the same questions that troubled them all night.

Popular advice to parents is simply "Just say no!" and MEAN it. This may work when your child is young, when she wants to stay out beyond curfew, when he wants you to pay for the most expensive cell phone on the market, when she wants to go to a party with people five years older than she is.

On the other hand, "Just say no!" is a piece of advice that can carry a hefty price tag, especially when you are dealing with an addict who is absolutely desperate to find his or her next fix. But this advice is bandied about, mainly by people who sit in comfortable offices and who will never have to pay the price for following that advice.

There was a time when I worked in the same school my sons attended and we all rode back and forth in the car together. From the highway en route, we had a beautiful view of a lovely farm nestled in a valley with a strip of blue-green mountains in the distance. On late afternoons, we saw the crimson and gold stripes of the sunset reflected off the tin roof of the barn and on fall mornings we watched the steam vaporize from the pond. We picked strawberries there one summer and stopped to take pictures of the farm on more than one occasion. One day we were reviewing vocabulary words in the car and Travis came upon the word "bucolic." The timing was perfect. I stopped the car along the side of highway and pointed to the farm. "This," I said, "is bucolic."

Some years later my husband came home from the local mini-mart visibly shaken. "You won't believe what happened," he said. "The owner from Worthington Farm went missing and when the police went looking, they found him and his son dead in the barn. I heard the police talking. Seems the son shot his father and then turned the gun on himself. Looking for money, they suspect. Drug money."

I pictured the barn, clean and bright in the sunlight, the silo nestled at its side. I shuddered to picture the scene the police discovered inside. And although it sounds like a cliché, it's really true. The father was an upstanding member of the community, on local community boards, always ready to donate or lend a helping hand. A good man by all accounts. Hundreds of people showed up at the wake. And a couple of weeks later, there was probably a therapist somewhere who looked at his watch and commented to his secretary, "Looks like Mr. Worthington forgot his appointment. Just charge him for a no-show."

One time I made an appointment for Daniel with a counselor in another city, a counselor who came highly recommended and with a correspondingly hefty hourly fee. He was, by all accounts, an expert in his field. I waited months for the appointment and was more than willing to pay his fee because I hoped he might be able to work some magic, provide fresh insight or have a connection that would move us a little closer to a solution. I was thrilled when Daniel said he would go, but since he and I would be coming to the session from different directions, he would need to get a ride with someone. Once again, I gave him money for a ride. Fifteen minutes past the designated time of the appointment, I was still alone in the waiting room of the counseling office flipping through outdated copies of *Field and Stream* and *Better Homes and Gardens*. When I finally reached Daniel by phone, his excuse was simply, "Something came up and I realized I couldn't make it there in time." And the reason you didn't call? "My phone wasn't charged." I wanted to scream in frustration.

Instead I asked to talk with the counselor. "Where is your son?" he asked abruptly, and I told him that apparently, he would not be coming. Perhaps we could call him by phone, I offered, but he told me that he didn't do phone counseling. But he appeased me by accepting me as a replacement client and in the minutes remaining in my time slot, I spilled out everything—the addiction, the chaos, the violence, the premonition that something bad awaited us, the frustration in not finding any solution. And this was his response: "You need to buckle up. Tough love. You just need to learn to say NO". And because he was so highly recommended and expensive, I decided to try his advice. I said NO. Plain and simple.

Sometime later his bill arrived in the mail. I looked at it for a few minutes and then fanaticized about responding with the following note: "I am returning your bill with the receipt for the $500 I paid to replace the window glass that shattered as a result of following your advice. I figure I have already paid for your advice. Let's just consider ourselves even."

People are quick to point their fingers at parents and caregivers and call them "enablers." This is not a descriptive word; it is a loaded word, as much as words like "loser" or "traitor" or "racist". In fact, some people can hardly say the word without sneering. And while avoiding enabling may be a well-intended guidance for parents, it butts up against the reality that when push comes to shove, parents and caregivers often trust their own natural and spiritual instincts more than advice and guidelines.

It may come as a surprise, but there is a lot of talk about God, or the "Higher Power," as He is sometimes called, in recovery circles. Many recovery centers, in fact, have been founded by religious groups, and God, or the "Higher Power," plays a pretty significant role in many organizations particularly Alcoholics Anonymous and Narcotics Anonymous. The addict is encouraged to seek deliverance from God, to pray, to turn his will over to the care of God. Sounds a lot like Christianity and other organized religions, doesn't it? And yet there is a complete disconnect around this issue. Recovery groups meet in the evenings in the basement of churches with a full pot of coffee brewing, and congregations meet on Sunday mornings in the vestibules upstairs with a coffee hour following the service. It's kind of a Downton Abbey model…two groups occupying the same place, in many cases praying to the same God, living entirely separate lives.

And there is that same strange disconnect regarding addicts and family members. Addicts are encouraged to let God or their "Higher Power" direct their paths according to His will and yet parents somehow are not. They are expected to follow a set of rules that have little to do with compassion or mercy, kindness or forgiveness. If you are Christian or Jewish or in any other religion that has clear-cut principles, you are asked to set aside those principles and follow another set of principles. There is a lot more talk about giving the problem to the professionals than there ever is about giving it to God or a Higher Power.

Parents have to walk a thin line all the time in deciding how and when to support and when to hold the line and insist on accountability. I think most parents try to preserve a relationship with their child even if they have been deceived or betrayed in every possible way. Keeping that connecting line, thin and frayed as it might be, may in the end be a lifeline, the rope their child reaches out for and latches onto in a desperate moment.

One young woman in recovery put it this way: "I am tired of hearing about tough love," she said. "I put my parents through terrible things, but I don't think I would be alive today if it weren't for their support. Addicts don't need tough love. They're already broken in so many ways. They need help to get themselves back together."

Parents give in to their children at times not because they are weak or pathetic or love too much or love too little. And it is not only to preserve a relationship with their child. Unless you have lived with someone with an addiction, it may be difficult to comprehend just how quickly situations can become intense, unpredictable and potentially dangerous. Parents give in because there is a priority that surpasses all others—safety. Anything else—money, cars, dishes, furniture—can be replaced. A human life cannot.

Some night when you are walking home alone at night and a stranger comes up to you and demands your money and your jewelry, just say No! and see where that gets you. No one does that—you quickly slip off your watch, your necklace, hand over your wallet, even offer up your precious cell phone—because instinctively you know that safety is paramount. You enable crime, you reinforce the thief by giving in; by giving in, you encourage him or her to try the same tactic again with some other victim. But when the police force gets together to discuss crime, no one points their fingers at the victims and accuses them of being enablers.

The first attorney we hired gave me an important piece of advice: *Learn to separate when the margarita is talking and when your son is.* It turned out to be a good survival technique even when our problems progressed from alcohol into drugs. It acted as a kind of armor that protected me from angry words and actions that might have otherwise hurt and antagonized me, destroyed our relationship altogether. It kept me from trying to reason with Daniel when he was under the influence and preserved a connection with the son I knew best, the one who appeared only occasionally but who I knew was there nonetheless. And suffering, maybe as much as I was.

The Enigma of Stigma

What I found amazing along the way is that there doesn't seem to be any consistent way of viewing an addict. Is the addict a victim or do we hold an addict entirely responsible for his or her actions? We know that addiction runs in families, like schizophrenia, diabetes or cancer and there is increasing evidence that it is a biological disorder, yet there is a unique stigma associated with addiction that isn't attached to other medical conditions.

With addiction, there seems to be some kind of punitive attitude, even after a person has gone through the whole process of recovery. *So you can't get a job, you can't get a decent apartment—so what? It's your own damn fault. You should have made better decisions.* There are few, if any, transition services available to a person in the initial phase of recovery. A person leaves a recovery program or jail with a resume that looks like swiss cheese, a lack of references, and perhaps a criminal record that will bar him from any subsidized housing or financial aid for college, even if it is a drug charge dating from years before. And if this isn't challenging enough, he or she faces the stigma that still encompasses addiction.

In fact, I first learned about this from students in the college class I teach. In one class, after I returned a set of papers, I noticed a student lingering behind to talk to me. I was surprised because this student hadn't spoken two words all semester, and I knew that he had received an A on the paper I had just returned. He waited until everyone left and then said, "I almost didn't turn this paper in to you. Do you think less of me now?" His paper had told the story of his struggle with addiction, time spent in jail and his eventual recovery years later. I looked him straight in the eye and said, "On the contrary. I think more of you now than I ever did." Another semester I had a student who wrote a paper and gave a presentation on nanotechnology. It was brilliant! It was the first time I felt I really had come to understand the whole field of nanotechnology. "I sure hope this is the field you're going into, because you will be a real asset to that field," I told him.

"I wish I could, but I'm not. I've talked to people in the field and they say I don't stand a chance. I have a record you see from years ago…drugs. I'm thinking maybe I'll go into addiction counseling… seems like the only career in which I have a chance of succeeding."

I hear more and more of these stories as the years go on. One of the assignments in the writing classes I teach is narration. Write me a story, I tell my students—simple as that. It doesn't have to be about something earth-shattering like death or love or accidents or cancer I tell them. I give them examples of stories about simple everyday things that have important inherent meaning, but when I get their papers two weeks later, they are inevitably about their major life story and increasingly over the years, they are about their own or a family member's struggle with addiction. After all, for many of them, *this is their story*. There is no other story quite as potent as this one. It is the story that they have told countless times at AA meetings, in outpatient group sessions, in Drug Court, in recovery programs. They are stories about shame, about relapse, about broken commitments and relationships, about life on the streets and time in jail, about the moment when they gained control of their lives and began to build a foundation for a different life. As a teacher, I struggle with these papers—what do you say when someone has poured out their heart, their most intimate story on paper and put it in your hands? *Nice story but too many run-on sentences? Good attention to detail but try to proof-read your work next time before handing it in?* As a fellow human being, I feel that I have been allowed to walk on holy ground, to peer into the world of miracles and transformation, to glimpse the strength of human will and prayer. I feel privileged and humbled that students have shared these stories with me.

After reading dozens and dozens of these stories, I have learned simply this: there may be some common threads, but each story is unique. Some people turned their life around because of a major event—a friend died of an overdose or in a car accident; their spouse filed for a divorce. But there are just as many who turned their life around because of a seemingly trivial event. One story I remember was from a young man who had been picked up on a DWI charge in the middle of the night. The police called his wife to pick him up at the station and she arrived with both their children still dressed in their pajamas, his son holding his wife's hand and hiding behind her leg, his daughter in his wife's arms, wearing a fleece bathrobe and pink bunny slippers. It was the pink bunny slippers that made all the difference for him. He burst into tears when he saw them; to him, the bunny slippers represented the purity and innocence of his young daughter who had been woken up and brought into stark, cold police station only because of his actions. That night was the beginning of sobriety for him. Would he still be drinking if his daughter had been wearing Velcro sneakers instead of slippers or if his wife had found someone to watch the kids so she could slip out alone in the middle of the night? I don't know. Other students had found commitment on top of a mountain or in a homeless shelter or in a prison cell or simply one sleepless night alone in their own living room as they watched the re-runs of their life story over and over again and decided it was time to change the channel. A deep-seated longing to escape addiction stirred by an insight or incident suddenly becomes the magic springboard for change.

Money and insurance coverage in most cases dictate the kind, duration and quality of treatment services for addiction. Some programs seem to have genuinely committed people earnestly trying to work with an addict's strengths, disabilities and personal challenges with an eye toward achieving the best possible short and long-term goal. They consider underlying factors such as ADHD, depression and other mental health disorders in working with the person. Some residential programs, on the other hand, are not much more than holding zones with caseworkers who earn little more than minimum wage and have few duties beyond keeping order. Yet there are success stories and failures from both kinds of organizations, I suppose, based on this: Organizations, after all, are made up of people and it is those people, not the organization itself, who often make the difference in any one person's life.

Some of the most agonizing stories I read are often those that come from parents, friends, siblings, husbands and wives and the struggles they go through trying to find some help for a loved one with an addiction, stories that grip me because they so often mirror my own journey. One story was particularly haunting. It was by a young girl whose sister had overdosed and died. "One life snuffed out," she wrote, "diminished the fire in all us. No holiday, no birthday, no family picnic in the backyard would ever be the same. She died a couple of years ago, but I still wonder, 'Did it really have to happen that way'?"

My heart ached for her as it does for all the people who have lost a loved one. I also find myself asking the same question: Did it really have to happen that way?

Of course, *I get it*…shortage of beds, cost of residential treatment, insurance restrictions, hospital policies, agency guidelines, tight budgets. There is always a reason to slam the door on someone else's problems. But what's the result? Addicts find themselves in the purgatory of peer counseling—listening to each other's stories for years at a time but never moving on to recovery. It's the classic game of Chutes and Ladders, forward and backward without ever reaching that final square on the gameboard.

Needless to say, the student essays about addiction and recovery which I read come from survivors. I often think of the others, the ones whose stories I may never read—those still in the throes of addiction, those who are already gone. Because as the years have gone on, the statistics regarding overdoses have become much more personal. They contain names that I know, faces that once sat at my supper table, players on Daniel's sport teams. They include people Jim and I have talked honestly with. "Why don't you try to get clean?" we'd ask. "You've a lot to gain and nothing to lose." And so often they'd say, "Good point. I'm planning to look into it, but not now…later" without realizing that there is a lot that can happen between now and later. Obituaries in the local papers are not just about people's grandparents; they are about young vibrant people who once looked forward to a future they will never know.

The world of addiction has long been shrouded in shame. It is only recently that parents have disclosed the cause of death in their child's obituary, mainly as a warning to others, a small way to bring some good out of a terrible, senseless death. As the old face of addiction is replaced by more familiar faces, the stigma of addiction is dissipating but not quickly enough. Research may point to addiction as a disease, but the idea that it comes from bad choices or a flawed character lingers on. Yet it is not as if the addict has been presented with a list of options and says yes! I think I'll choose the option that will lead to self-degradation, broken relationships, hardship and heartache. I choose the one that may lead to jail, may cause me to lose my children, may result in a life of crime and hardship, may lead to an early death. Yes! Addiction! That's the one for me!

Of course not. Addiction takes a more insidious course. People undergo a surgery, perhaps have a sports injury and innocently take prescription medication for the pain. Injury healed, prescription ended, they suddenly realize that they cannot imagine a reality that does not include that drug. Or they simply follow along with what their friends do; they *try* something just for kicks and while their friends say, "not for me" and walk away, they are somehow hooked. A little further down the road, they lose control of the wheel and find it is the drugs that are now driving their actions and they are just along for the ride.

And it is no joy ride, believe me. Because at the same time an addict will steal, manipulate or throw anyone under the bus to get the next fix, there is the unsettling awareness that something important has been violated in their lives—order, values, common decency. That is the bitter pill that comes in the cocktail with the other drugs, and ironically it is these same values that often become the pivotal point of change: *I stopped drinking because I didn't want my daughter to see me as a falling down drunk. I didn't want to spend the rest of my life knowing that everyone I care about was ashamed of me. I looked at myself and discovered that I had become everything I hated about other people.*

I knew that Daniel wasn't happy with his own life. I knew he felt guilty about all the pain he had caused and ashamed that he had violated principles that at one time had guided his actions. His inner world was in turmoil but that didn't seem to be enough to loosen the grip that addiction had on him.

One day, however, Daniel opened a window into his inner world and kindled a hope in mine. I was riding in the car (where else?) with him through one of our nearby cities when suddenly he grabbed my arm and said: "Slow down a minute. Look over there," and he pointed to a couple of young men his age walking down the street together, talking and laughing. "That's what I want. That's what I dream of, a simple uncomplicated ordinary life. Look at them…just a couple of friends meeting up on a Friday afternoon after work, going out to hang out somewhere and have a few laughs." I looked again at the two young men and then back at Daniel. Perhaps it was setting the bar a little low, but I understood what he was saying. He was yearning for the *normal*, something he hadn't done in years.

A Very Present Help

As long as our journey had lasted, the end came swiftly. It was like being on a high-speed terrifying train ride that suddenly jolts to a halt for no apparent reason at all. One morning as I was getting ready for work, Daniel announced that he needed a ride to probation. I could hear Jim groaning in the background. I was suspicious too. All too often, so-called appointments had been a ploy to get one of us in a car with a motive that had nothing to do with probation. I called the probation office to verify the appointment as I had done so many times in the past. I didn't even need to identity myself; I had called so often the receptionist immediately recognized my voice. Daniel, as it turned out, did have an appointment that morning. Again, the debate began over who would skip work to drive him there. It happened to be a Thursday, a day that was sacred in my job. You might be violently ill, but you were still expected to arrive at the weekly Thursday meeting, no matter if you had to arrive in a wheelchair with an oxygen tank attached or by ambulance. I had never missed one of those meetings, nor had any of those meetings ever been cancelled. And yet, for whatever reason, the meeting that morning was cancelled, so I reluctantly offered to take Daniel.

This was naturally a happy solution for Jim, who could now go on with his day, but it left me with a sense of foreboding. Before he left, Jim warned me of possible ulterior motives involved, as if I needed the warning. I was anticipating a miserable ride, with squabbles over money for the day and places Daniel needed to be. Nevertheless, I started the car, Daniel climbed in and off we went. Sort of. Two minutes down the road, he announced he needed to pay back a debt before going, and so the arguments began. I was tempted to just pull over, turn around and give up on the trip to probation. But I didn't. It turned out that he needed only $20, the house he needed to go to was on our way and now that I had already called in late to work, I was determined to get him to his appointment, once and for all. The short stop along the way put us behind schedule, so the arguments switched to my driving.

"Speed up. I can't be late to this appointment."

"I'm not speeding, just because you insisted on paying back someone," I muttered, but inwardly I prayed we would avoid hitting any red lights, which would save us some time along the way. Green lights the whole way, as it turned out. We pulled into the parking lot, just on the dot of nine, right on time. He climbed out, I stayed in the car and tried to calculate what time I might make it back to work. The same old routine. But, as it turned out, we were on a different track this time. A few minutes after Daniel got out of the car, he jumped back in and announced we needed to go to court. Drug Court.

Drug Court? This was one of the doors that had been closed to us in the past. Permanently, I thought. Was this a possibility that Daniel might be able to get into some kind of treatment program? After so many dashed expectations, I didn't want to get my hopes up.

"Are you sure?"

"That's what they told me. But not now. Later. First I need to go to the police station in town and get a copy of my fingerprints."

Well, there went any thought of getting to work some time that morning. I turned the car around and headed back home, grumbling the whole way. *Later*. I hate *later*. *Later* is always an opportunity for something to go wrong.

And it did. When I arrived at the police station, the door was locked and no one answered the doorbell. The alternative was to call 911, which didn't seem appropriate at the time. We waited and we waited, and finally Daniel insisted he wanted to go home and we could try again later in the day. I dropped him off and decided to go back to see if anyone had arrived at the station, but just as I got there, my phone rang. It was someone from Drug Court. "Did your son tell you that you need to be back here by 12:00?"

"Noooo." 12:00 noon sounded a lot more like *sooner* than *later*. I rang the bell at the police station over and over, just on the odd chance that someone inside would get annoyed enough to answer the door. But the door remained shut. Suddenly, I remembered that months before someone had given me an "inside" number for the police department which I had jotted down on a slip of paper. Where was this number now? I vaguely remember bringing it into the house, but quickly browsed through my glove compartment and my wallet, hoping I might have had the good sense to put it somewhere handy. No such luck. And then I noticed a scrap of paper on the floor of the passenger side of the car, picked it up and turned it over. *There it was,* the magic number. I dialed it and someone answered immediately. The person on the other end of the line was more than helpful. He gave me the exact location of the police officer on duty, a place I recognized and just a few miles from where I was parked. Hurrah! I took a quick detour to stop at the restroom of a mini-mart along the way before heading on to the main road. I was just about to pull into the parking lot when, to my amazement, I realized that the car pulling out of the parking area was in fact the local police car. He pulled onto the main road and I pulled around behind him. In full pursuit, I glanced at my speedometer and realized that I was now driving over the speed limit. *Can you get booked for speeding by chasing a speeding police car?* I didn't care at that point. I was on a roll. A door had cracked open and I was determined to keep my foot in it before it slammed shut.

I followed the policeman into the station and quickly explained my situation.

"Fingerprints?" he said. "It generally takes 5 to 7 days to get fingerprints. When do you need them?"

"Now," I said. "I need to be in the courthouse with them in about an hour."

Whether he responded to the sound of desperation in my voice or whether he feared he would have to babysit me in his office for the rest of the morning, he picked up the phone and dialed.

"Hey, bud," he said to whoever was on the other end of the line. "I think you owe me a favor. I've got this lady here in my office who says she needs to have a set of fingerprints to go to court in an hour. Yeah, yeah, I know. But is there any chance you could just drop what you're doing and take care of this?"

In the middle of his conversation, my cell phone rang and I recognized the same number that had called before. Drug Court again. The woman on the other end of the line wasn't sure she had given Daniel the right information about what she needed. I passed the phone to the police officer and let them talk. Eventually he handed the phone back to me. "Remember you need to be here by 12:00 or the whole thing is off," the woman said.

The whole thing? We had *a thing*? What did that mean? Could it possibly mean…? For a moment there, it was as if the Red Sea had opened. Before I could ask for details, she hung up the phone. And there was no time to waste at this point anyway. I thanked the police officer, headed home to pick up Daniel and we were back on the road to the courthouse again.

We arrived right on time and the coordinator, the voice of my phone call, was there to meet us. The first order of business was a drug test which naturally came up dirty. *Surprise, surprise.* "And whatever you took," she mentioned, "was laced with something else." I could tell by his expression that this information came as a surprise to Daniel. "You're damn lucky you're alive, you know that?" I had heard this comment to Daniel so many times, from police officers, from lawyers, from probation officers, that I forgot to look shocked.

And while Daniel waited on a bench outside the courtroom, she took me aside and told me that Daniel was scheduled to go into treatment the following day. I simply nodded, stunned. "Do you think he is a flight risk?" she asked. "Because there is a possibility we could keep him until then."

I knew exactly what she meant by "keeping him". I took a quick look at Daniel, fidgeting on the bench, constantly glancing at the door to the outside and made a quick mental calculation: Daniel was impulsive, he didn't want to go into treatment and had expressed on any number of occasions that he'd run off rather than face involuntary treatment. He was already eyeing the door. This was a no-brainer. Using words that I never in my life expected to utter but which I have never regretted to this day, I said simply: "Lock him up."

And that is what happened. He went directly from the courthouse to jail and went directly from jail into a treatment facility the following day. Jim and I met him at the jail in the morning to give him a suitcase with assorted clothes, a pack of cigarettes and a few encouraging words. Daniel was still dressed in the clothes from the day before and looked exhausted. We were hardly better off: we were still in shock and operating on a fitful night of sleep. I will forever remember the deep searching look Daniel gave me as he waited for the car which would take him to the treatment facility to pull up to the curb. *What now? What now?*

I knew how much he feared detox, how unsettling it was for him to be wrenched from his normal routine, miserable as it was, and within 24 hours go from probation to court to jail and to a treatment center without so much as a change of clothes. I was reminded of the time that I had taken him and Travis tubing down a river in the

Catskill Mountains. It was a dumb decision on my part. I didn't know there were both rocks and rapids along the way, and this was far too challenging a ride for children that young. None of us had even bothered to put on life jackets. But both boys had jumped into their tubes and were swiftly moving downstream before I could do anything to stop them. Travis was already ahead of us and I was doing my best to catch up to him when I heard a wail from behind. "MAAAAH!" It was the voice of sheer panic. I looked back and saw that Daniel had lost his tube and was being swept downstream on his own. I quickly braced myself against the nearest boulder I could find and reached out for him as he zoomed by. Miraculously, I managed to grab hold of the tube and then Daniel as they swept by me. When I looked downstream, to my relief, I saw that Travis had maneuvered himself to the side of the river and had managed to get himself and his tube onto the bank. With Travis safe, Daniel and I huddled there at the rock in the freezing water, hanging onto our tubes and each other for a few minutes, watching the water rush swiftly by us. Danger averted. One of those bonding moments you never forget.

There was no wailing cry this time, but I saw the same look of panic in Daniel's eyes. We were all caught up in the current, but this time, there would be no reaching out to save him. "You'll be OK. You can do this," I heard Jim tell him. Daniel shrugged his shoulders and said nothing. The driver pulled the car in front and opened the door. It was time to go. Jim handed the suitcase to Daniel and with one final hug, I offered him the best words I could think of at the time. "You're not alone in this, Daniel. If God brought you to this moment in time, He will be with you through the whole process. Don't you forget that." And he was gone.

ALL ABOARD!

We stayed there in the parking area watching the car until it pulled onto the main road. There didn't seem to be much to say. We had just sent our son off with a stranger to a place we knew almost nothing about and an experience we knew even less about.

"Driver seemed a nice enough guy," Jim said as we got in our car. A comforting thought.

He dropped me off at home and left for work, although I later learned he had spent the day driving aimlessly, pondering the whole sequence of events. It took me less than ten seconds to decide that I wasn't going to work that day, and another five to decide I wasn't about to spend the day doing anything productive either. I settled into my old chair in the back yard, no longer staring into the abyss, but nestled in the world of awe. If the tree above me had suddenly sprinkled down fairy dust, I would not have been surprised. I thought about my cancelled meeting, the sudden appearance of the phone number, the "chance" encounter with the police car, the phone call in the police station and other strange details of the day. I thought of all the dead-ends, detours and disappointments over the years and tried to find the link between them and the last twenty-four hours. There was just no way to connect the dots. All the years filled with struggle, frustration and anguish and then one day, not much different from any other day, a path was suddenly swept clear, as if by a mere swish of a hand, and suddenly we woke up to a world that made sense again. It was Thanksgiving Day without the turkey.

I was still sitting there when Jim returned. He pulled up a chair next to me and we just sat there together for a while. I had called him from the courthouse the previous day and tried to give him the basic sequence of events as best as I could, but it wasn't until we stood in the parking lot outside the jail and watched Daniel drive off that the reality of the whole situation hit home. Thousands of prayers asking for just this moment, yet when it came, it came as a total surprise.

"What just happened?" Jim finally asked.

"I was going to ask you the same thing." And we continued to sit there, lost in our own thoughts.

"Think he'll make it?"

"God doesn't do things half-way, does he?"

"I suppose not."

But still I caught myself listening for the sound of the front door opening, footsteps on the stairs, familiar music coming from his room. The house stayed deathly quiet, empty. I felt as if a tremendous weight had been lifted from me, but without knowing what was going on with Daniel, I found myself trapped in a kind of holding pattern. Work, grocery shopping, dinner, maybe a movie or TV. Safety in routines. I called Travis and a couple of friends just to let them know the news and we waited. We had read online that there would be no phone contact with clients for the first month, so we were surprised one day when we picked up the phone and heard Daniel's voice. He wanted to let us know that he was fine. The detox process, which he feared would kill him, was over in two days. "Can you believe it?" he asked. The food wasn't bad, he had made friends, liked his counselor. Could we send him some sweat pants because he had started working out and wanted to start running. Would we be coming for the Family Day next month?

It was not the family visiting day we had always anticipated, but somehow that didn't seem so important anymore. "We'll be there," I told him. "Wild horses couldn't keep us away.' And he laughed.

Letters went back and forth, and more and more we recognized the Daniel we had known years before. "Can you send more Jolly Rancher candy?" he asked in another phone call. "As big a bag as you can find. They're like currency here." His sense of humor was back. It occurred to me that it had been a long time since I had heard his laughter. Ironically, I felt more at home with him now than I had felt when he was at home.

Mind the Gap between the train and the Platform

Not long after Daniel went into treatment, the focus on opiate addiction intensified. Too many deaths hitting too close to home. Alarms went off in communities across the country, alarms too loud to ignore. Politicians began to include opiate addiction in their campaign speeches. Medical researchers began weighing in on the problem. The media expanded their coverage. Community meetings and committees sprang up all over the country.

With Daniel in treatment, I had more time available to attend some of these meetings, to follow media coverage. I was surprised to discover that while the nation may have come together in recognizing the magnitude of the problem, states and communities were determined to address it in their own individual way. Some states chose to stiffen punishments for users, others to relax them. Some promoted medically assisted treatment while others pushed for additional detox facilities. Many chose to divert funds toward prevention. Few chose to allocate funds for transition services or support for people in early stages of recovery. I distinctly remember one meeting at which a presenter reassured the public who had gathered that the problem with addiction in the community had already been addressed. There were no residential programs, detox units or suboxone doctors in the area but they had had a counseling program in place for years. "Why re-invent the wheel?" he asked rhetorically. *Why?! Because your wheel is broken,* I wanted to shout. *It has a flat tire. How about that for an answer!*

One meeting in particular, however, caught my attention. It took place in a small town in a county that had experienced several deaths from drug overdose. Community members gathered in the local high school to share ideas and listen to the local police chief describe the program he was proposing. The first thing he said was that he considered himself an addict, which surprised many of us, a recovered alcoholic to be exact. The second thing he said was that in putting together a program to confront addiction in the community, everyone had a voice at the table—community members, police, providers, parents, spouses, the addicts themselves. I had to restrain myself from interrupting him with thunderous applause at that point. Everyone had a role to play in the recovery process, he continued, not only treatment providers. Yes, there was a shortage of beds in the area, he admitted, but they would find a bed in inpatient treatment for anyone who needed one, whatever it took. And if anyone came to the police station or approached any of their officers looking for help with addiction, he or she would find it without facing criminal charges. There was no stigma attached to seeking help, no lecture about bad decisions and lifestyles—just a chance to move onward. I was impressed and so were many others. There was hope and a genuine commitment to helping solve the problem. The program met with almost immediate success. People with an addiction to substances found the help they needed when they needed it. *Imagine!* And they started down the path to recovery. And more and more people kept coming, from their community, from neighboring communities, from communities across the state where no help was available.

I think there is a lesson here. Maybe we need to look to these kinds of innovative approaches to stem the tide of addiction. It is not just users who are affected by addiction—it is all of us. Hurricanes, floods, tornados and fires all elicit our attention: we cannot help but be moved by the vivid images captured by the media and we instinctively reach out to help those whose lives have been devastated. Is it such a stretch to think that we could reach out in that same way to all those whose lives have been devastated by addiction?

The increased focus on addiction has prompted changes long overdue: better control over opiate prescriptions, narcan trainings, increased access to suboxone and other replacement drugs, stepped-up outreach and prevention programs—but it shouldn't stop there. Maybe we need to go deeper than this. Maybe we need to be willing to discard ineffective models of treatment, unshackle ourselves from old patterns of thought, revise agency policies, embrace community and family resources, and change the appalling rate of recidivism by providing some genuine help to those just starting out on the road to recovery. Genuine help goes beyond talk—it means help finding a decent place to live and a reliable job; help finding a new network of friends, a mentor or support group; help building the foundation for a life in recovery, a life with dignity and promise. Who knows? Maybe we need to let the people meeting in the church basements know that they are always welcome on the upper floor. Not easy, maybe, but a good start.

Amazing Grace

F amily Visiting Day at Daniel's facility was far more than I anticipated or could have wished for. What can I say? Daniel had blossomed during the time he was there. He was more animated, easy-going, happy. His hours running and on the exercise machines had paid off—he even *looked* different. "Remember the last words you said to me, Mom?" he asked at one point. "It all happened just as you said it would." I thought perhaps he would expand on this, but instead he went on to recite a list of things we could send him in the mail. "Hair cream, body wash, warm clothes, I'm going to need warm clothes soon. Oh! and Jolly Ranchers candy, did I mention more Jolly Ranchers?" I just shook my head. My son Daniel.

It was the opening pages of a new chapter. Recovery, as I was to learn, was not an event, but rather a process. There would be bumps along the path ahead, scars to heal, challenges to face, and relationships to rebuild, but we would all face them with a greater assurance. It was not only Daniel who had changed; Jim and I had changed also. We closed that chapter of our lives with far more compassion, understanding and patience that we had when we started our journey. People who learn of our story are quick to tell us how lucky we are. Grateful, yes. Lucky, no. Because I know now that even in our bleakest moments, when I could see nothing but emptiness all around me, there was one who stood with us, all along the way.

ABOUT THE AUTHOR

Lynda Hacker Araoz spent years trying to help her son recover from a heroin addiction. She has lived the majority of her life in upstate New York and Buenos Aires, Argentina where she has worked as a counselor, adolescent therapist, school administrator and teacher. She has a Master's Degree in Social Work from SUNY-Albany and another in English from University of Birmingham (UK).

Lynda lives with her husband Carlos and is currently an Adjunct Faculty member at Hudson Valley Community College and a volunteer at Pathways to Recovery.

Morgan James
Speakers Group

www.TheMorganJamesSpeakersGroup.com

We connect Morgan James published
authors with live and online events
and audiences who will benefit
from their expertise.